W9-CLG-188

# KENNETH DRAKE

# THE SONATAS OF
# Beethoven

## *as he played and taught them*

EDITED BY

# Frank S. Stillings

MUSIC TEACHERS NATIONAL ASSOCIATION • CINCINNATI

TO

*my mother and father*

# Foreword

NEAR THE END of his life, Beethoven remarked to young Gerhard von Breuning that he had once considered writing a piano method. From Schindler we learn that the intention to write such a text was related to a proposed new edition of Beethoven's works, a project which also never materialized, even though it occupied Beethoven's mind for a period of at least ten years. If the plan had been carried out, both projects might have been combined into one large instructive work dealing with the performance of Beethoven's works.

Fortunately, Beethoven's energies were consumed in bringing forth new works; he did not possess a mind for codifying teaching and performing procedures. He had no patience with voluminous piano methods and, therefore, chose for Gerhard the shortest of the current texts, Clementi's *Introduction to the Art of Playing the Piano Forte.* Lacking a piano method by Beethoven, the best contemporary guide to the performance of his works is the information provided by his pupils. The latter may in fact be more valuable than such a method because of the benefit derived from a study of differing viewpoints.

A serious student of Beethoven should have the following books in his library: (1) *Thayer's Life of Beethoven,* revised and edited by Elliot Forbes and published in two volumes in 1967 and in a one-volume paperback in 1970 by Princeton University Press; (2) Anton Schinder's *Beethoven as I Knew Him,* edited by the late Donald MacArdle and published by the University of North Carolina Press in 1966: (3) Carl Czerny's *Ueber den richtigen Vortrag der Sämtlichen Beethoven'schen Klavierwerke* ("On the Correct Performance of the Complete Beethoven Piano Works"), recently published in English by Universal with commentary by Paul Badura-Skoda; and (4) Carl Philipp Emanuel Bach's *Versuch über die wahre Art, das Clavier zu spielen* ("Essay on the True Art of Playing Keyboard Instruments"), translated and edited by William J. Mitchell and published by W. W. Norton. In the case of each work, the reader will find the sizable body of editorial notes and introductory comment highly informative.

Permission to reproduce the Czerny-Simrock metronome markings for the Sonatas from Badura-Skoda's supplementary notes to the Czerny *Ueber den richtigen Vortrag* . . . was granted by the publisher, Universal Edition. The Bülow markings are given by permission of G. Schirmer, and the Schnabel metronome markings, taken from his edition of the Sonatas (1935), are included by permission of the publisher, Simon and Schuster. All quotations from the Czerny *Ueber den richtigen Vortrag* . . . (Chapters 2 and 3 of Volume IV of his *Pianoforte Schule, Op.* 500), as well as those from Ries, Breuning, Marx, Nottebohm, and Kalischer, are my own translations of the German text.

In addition to the permissions mentioned above, the following publishers have kindly granted permission for the use of specific quotations found in this study:

The University of North Carolina Press, Chapel Hill; Faber and Faber Ltd., London (Anton Schindler, *Beethoven as I Knew Him*)

St. Martin's Press, New York (Emily Anderson, *The Letters of Beethoven*)

Princeton University Press, Princeton (*Thayer's Life of Beethoven*)

Dover Publications, New York (O. G. Sonneck, *Beethoven: Impressions by His Contemporaries;* and Friedrich Kerst, *Beethoven: The Man and the Artist as Revealed in his own Words*)

W. W. Norton and Company, New York (C. P. E. Bach, *Essay on the True Art of Playing Keyboard Instruments*)

Philosophical Library, New York (Roy Pascal, *The German Sturm und Drang*)

In the case of each quotation, the appropriate author, title, editor and translator (if any), publisher, date of publication and page is indicated in Notes and Sources at the end of the chapter.

By way of explanation, the roman numeral following the opus number above each example indicates the movement from which the example is taken. The numbers following the movement numeral indicate the measure or measures included in the example. An opus and number combination is reduced to two numbers separated by a slash, thus: Opus 2 number 3 becoming Op. 2/3. The abbreviation WoO stands for "Without Opus," the number which follows being that given in the Kinsky *Verzeichnis* of Beethoven's works.

I am deeply grateful to Nadine Dresskell of Arizona State University for her suggestion that this study be published by the MUSIC TEACHERS NATIONAL ASSOCIATION, to Willis F. Ducrest of University of Southwestern Louisiana and the members of the *MTNA* Development Commission for their subsequent interest in carrying out the plan, and to Dr. Frank S. Stillings of Central Michigan University for his patience and careful attention to my manuscript as Editor. I wish to express appreciation also for assistance given by Dr. Nicholas Temperley of the University of Illinois in the original preparation of the text, as well as to Dean Paul J. Jackson for his suggestions on Chapter VIII. Finally, I owe a debt of gratitude to those with whom I studied: Eskil Randolph, now an *MTNA* member in Portland, Oregon, whose early training has remained a determining influence in my work, Stanley Fletcher, whose musical guidance and professional assistance have been an inestimable help, to Grete Hinterhofer of the Vienna Akademie, to the late José Echaniz, to remember whom as a musician and a friend is always a moving experience.

Kenneth Drake
*March, 1972*

# The Sonatas
# of Beethoven

# Contents

# I

# The Teacher
# and His Students

MUSIC IS a performing art and, consequently, as the person plays, or would like to play, so he also teaches. For this reason it is essential to reconstruct a concept of Beethoven the performer as he understood performance, using recorded comment and information dealing with the practices and attitudes of his time. This body of information suggests four approaches to an understanding of Beethoven's playing: his early musical training, the thinking of the German *Sturm und Drang* ("Storm and Stress"), Beethoven's piano, and his manner of improvisation. To appreciate the contrast between the values and standards of Beethoven's generation and our own, one question should be kept in mind, "How would the professional musician of today have fared in those circumstances?"

**Beethoven's Early Musical Training.** — Like the young Mozart, Beethoven began his study with his father. Beyond this, the similarity in early study ends. Although Johann van Beethoven was held in esteem at the electoral court in Bonn, he was neither the person nor the teacher that Leopold Mozart was. Later in life, in conversations with Czerny and Schindler, Beethoven complained bitterly about the inconsistent, inadequate training he had received from his father, pointing out that Mozart's success was in no small measure due to Leopold Mozart's orderly, thorough preparation.[1] Moreover, a lack of rapport between the young Beethoven and his father, the result of the boy's withdrawn manner and his father's mistrust, made an effective working relationship impossible. Since punishment only widened the gulf between them, and since Johann was primarily a voice teacher, he eventually decided to turn over the guidance of his

1

son to someone else. The teachers with whom Beethoven studied thereafter, prior to the arrival of Christian Gottlob Neefe, may well be passed over in silence. They were, in Schiedermair's words, the "most dissimilar individuals,"[2] and Beethoven had the additional disadvantage of being subjected to each one for a relatively short period of time.

Neefe arrived in Bonn at a critical point in Beethoven's development, both in a personal and in an artistic sense. Personally, he was warm and unpretentious, earning Beethoven's respect by demanding of himself the same dedication to thoroughness and hard work that he required of his student. With respect to artistic matters, Neefe's influence was undeniably important, even crucial, in helping the young Beethoven chart his musical course. First of all, Neefe was responsible for introducing Beethoven to the *Well-Tempered Clavier* (at a time when the musical world was only beginning to rediscover this work) and to Philipp Emanuel Bach's *Essay on the True Art of Playing Keyboard Instruments.* As might be expected, Beethoven's study with Neefe was not the sort of specialized training which is usual in the studio today; the study of a keyboard instrument included practice in realizing figured bass and a knowledge of composition, not just the mastering of the instrument's technical problems. The private teacher of Beethoven's day had to be all the departments of the present-day conservatory in one person. In Neefe's case this all-around competence as a professional musician was most impressive, considering the variety of assignments required of him in the theatrical group with which he was associated: coaching, directing, translating Italian and French opera texts, serving as court organist, playing cembalo in the court concerts, and teaching. Apart from these duties he also found time to be a poet, a biographer, and a contributor to professional journals. Finally, Neefe's evaluations of other musicians in Bonn and at the court reveal the attitudes toward performance which he stressed in his teaching. *Capelldirektor* Mattioli, Neefe wrote, had introduced a declamatory style and strict regard for dynamic nuances in the orchestra.[3] Countess von Hatzfeld surrendered herself to her emotions at the piano, as a result of which her playing often exhibited tempo *rubato,* although without becoming unsteady. Another amateur played clavier and violin, if not skillfully, with "very correct musical feeling."[4] Of himself, Neefe admitted that he could not compose when not in the mood and that, on those occasions when he had been required to do so, he preferred to disown the result.[5]

Declamatory performance, the exploitation of dynamic shading, yielding oneself to one's emotions, tempo *rubato* within a steady tempo, "correct" musical feeling, performances which are dependent upon moods and are therefore uneven — all are characteristics of Beethoven's own manner of playing and teaching reflected in the reports of his students and contemporaries.

**Sturm und Drang.** — It was through his association with Neefe and the members and friends of the Breuning family that the brooding, complex young Beethoven was drawn into the current of contemporary philosophical thought.

> Thus, with the children growing up and the household circle enlarged by the arrival of intelligent youths from outside the home [Wegeler and Beethoven], the life and activity in the house became more intense, and all the more so, as a common press for knowledge associated with the lively influence exerted by the spreading reforms of the literature of the period inspired all the young people of the house.[6]

The "spreading reforms" of literature to which Gerhard von Breuning referred were those of the German literary movement of the 1770's, the Storm and Stress. Although the Storm and Stress was the spiritual heir of the writings of Rousseau, for Rousseau, also, the ideas were already there, surrounding him in the thinking of the society in which he moved and reflecting its interest in primitive happiness and the appeal of exotic, distant places. In *The Question of Jean-Jacques Rousseau,* Ernst Cassirer depicts Rousseau as a spokesman of his age against his age, challenging the power of intellectualism with the "irresistible primitive force" of feeling.[7]

A tendency exists to believe that abstract ideas have little practical value in playing the piano or in teaching. As a result, the playing heard in the studio often bears a resemblance to the mouthing of lines memorized without a knowledge of their context within the play. To understand the parallels between the thinking of the Storm and Stress and Beethoven is to hear the music within the context of the ideas which gave it life. For amplification two works of Goethe, *Die Leiden des jungen Werthers* and *Faust,* will suffice to illustrate these parallels.

*The Sorrows of Young Werther* is the story of a love triangle, told in the form of a series of letters from Werther to a friend. In the letters Werther describes his meeting with Lotte, with whom he falls deeply in love but who is already engaged to marry another man. The plot is relatively unimportant. The significant aspect of the story is that it deals with the force of human passion, which, in this case, is consummated in Werther's suicide. In Goethe's *Faust,* Mephistopheles offers his powers to Faust in return for Faust's service in the next world. In concluding the bargain, Faust says, in effect: "If you can make me content with myself or satisfied with the pleasure and beauty of the present moment, then I will be finished, and you will be freed from your service." Faust, wanting to experience life afresh, is changed by Mephistopheles into a vigorous young man whose passion for Gretchen destroys the innocent wholesomeness of her life. As a consequence of her deepening affair with Faust, she is driven to the murder of her mother and her child. In the final scene, incoherent and awaiting execution, Gretchen is visited in prison by a Faust who is filled with remorse. As Mephistopheles leads him away in despair, a "voice from above" declares, "She is saved!"

Both Werther and Faust are possessed by the desire for deeper personal experience, even though the consequence of their actions is the undoing of the individual each loves. Speaking of this pattern, Roy Pascal writes that

> . . . in his greatest works Goethe persuades us that in break-ing the bounds of society and morality, his heroes discover a deeper meaning in life, a fullness and richness unknown to those who observe external codes. This highest intensity of being is the extreme of individualism but at the same time its dissolution, its self-loss in feeling . . . [8]

Based on evidence provided in the comments of his contemporaries, Beethoven, beyond any doubt, subscribed to these sentiments. Clementi said of his playing, for instance, that it was often violent — as Beethoven himself was — and lacking in finish, although it was always soulful. As Beethoven played, so he also taught, according to Ries:

> If I missed something in a passage or incorrectly played notes and leaps which he wanted to have consistently accur-ate, he seldom said anything; only if I showed a lack in ex-

pression, in *crescendi,* etc., or in the character of the piece did he become aroused, because, he said, the former is an accident, the latter a lack of knowledge, feeling, or attention. The former happened quite often to him, even when he played in public.[9]

Cherubini was less charitable, characterizing Beethoven's playing as "rough"[10] . . . *il est toujours brusque.*[11]

Unlike a trained virtuoso who practices to make himself independent of moods, Beethoven depended upon the combination of his enormous musical gift and the intensity of his subjective feelings at the moment to overcome technical problems. Using almost the exact same words as Pascal, who wrote that Goethe "found the sense of life in 'surrendering himself from moment to moment,' even though this brought torment as well as rapture,"[12] Czerny spoke of the "moods to which he [Beethoven] surrendered himself," adding that as a consequence, even "if it were possible to reproduce his playing manner exactly, it could not (in relation to the present development of polish and clarity) always serve as a model . . . ."[13] According to Schindler, it was not so much the lack of polish as the inconsistency of performance governed by moods — the same work brilliant and spirited one day, "muddled" the next — to which Cramer objected.[14]

Individualism at any price may explain the original fast tempo marking ( $\d = 138$ ) for the first movement of the Sonata, Op. 106. Playing the movement at that tempo might mar the performance, although for Beethoven the spirit of the piece could only be found by attempting the impossible. Individualism need not always result in dissolution. Just as Goethe chose an individualistic manner of presenting the narrative of Werther by having the main character tell his experiences in the first person, one reads of the "rhetorical" quality of Beethoven's playing. As one who always played "in the first person," Beethoven must have been in full agreement with C.P.E. Bach's statement in the *Essay,* "A musician cannot move others unless he too is moved."[15]

One of the significant accomplishments of the Storm and Stress, according to Pascal, is "the fusion of imaginative experience and reality."[16] *Werther* was based upon an incident in Goethe's life, Werther being Goethe, and Lotte, in real life, Charlotte Buff, the fiancée of a friend of Goethe. An analogy from everyday life was frequently utilized by Beethoven in teaching to provide psychological suggestion, by mean of which the impression which incited his creative process could be shared with the performer:

> . . . the Largo of Op. 10/3 suggesting through nuances of dynamic shading the mental state of a person in a deeply depressed mood. (Schindler)[17]

> . . . the Adagio of Op. 27/2 like a "night scene, where a plaintive voice sounds from a great distance." (Czerny)[18]

> . . . the theme of the finale of Op. 31/2 having been improvised by Beethoven after seeing a rider gallop past his window. (Czerny)[19]

> . . . the finale of Op. 57 like "the waves of the sea on a stormy night, while from afar a call for help is heard." (Czerny)[20]

> . . . the first and third movements of Op. 101 characterized by Beethoven as "Impressions and Reveries." (Schindler)[21]

The importance that Beethoven placed upon this type of psychological suggestion is revealed in Schindler's statement that one of Beethoven's motives for wanting to prepare a new edition of his piano works was the desire to reveal the extra-musical idea behind each composition.[22]

Finally, the creative spirit of the times went to the commonplace and the everyday for its raw material. Characters from the middle and lower classes of society figure prominently in works of the Storm and Stress, in which the tension within their lives between normal behavior and emotional stress gives their personalities, attitudes and speech dramatic significance. According to reports of his improvisations, Beethoven typically began with simple ideas, giving this material psychological meaning through his style of playing and discovering a theme as he progressed. The result is evident in many Beethoven scores in which a theme has retained the outlines of its origin in a simple pattern — a broken chord or a scale segment. A Leipzig critic writing about the "Eroica" found this disturbing, saying that one should not converse about everyday matters overlong or in an obscure manner.[23]

A poem of Goethe, *Selige Sehnsucht* ("Blessed Yearning"), expresses the spirit of the Storm and Stress in a few short lines. Man, the poet says, must be consumed in experience like a moth which

is drawn into the flame of a candle, and, unless he has this desire
to die and be transformed, he will remain a dull guest on a dark
earth.[24]

**Beethoven's Piano.** — Without an awareness of the spirit of the
times discussed above, the true import of the construction and
sound of Beethoven's piano cannot be fully understood. Even if one
could hear a piano of Beethoven's time exactly as it sounded when
it left the builder's shop, having heard the modern piano, any
judgment would be prejudiced. Furthermore, to say that Beethoven
was writing for the modern piano is as relevant to an understanding
of his treatment of the piano as it would be to speculate on the
outcome of the Revolutionary War had it been fought with modern
instruments of warfare. The piano of that time possessed certain
qualities and presented certain problems which influenced Beethoven's keyboard style. Before an audience, the success or failure of
such an instrument depends upon the performer's response to "facts
of life" peculiar to Beethoven's piano: the levels of sound and
the tone quality of each, and to a lesser degree, compass and durability.

The generally smaller sound which one associates with an old
instrument is due to several factors: lighter stringing, lower string
tension, and smaller hammers. In actuality, the dynamic range may
be just as wide as that of a modern piano, although, having heard
our contemporary pianos all our lives, there is a tendency to equate
only loudness with dynamic range. The relative effect of the dynamic
levels possible on each instrument might be visualized as follows:

| PIANO OF TODAY | PIANO OF BEETHOVEN'S PERIOD |
|:---:|:---:|
| *fff* | |
| *ff* | |
| *f* | *ff* |
| *mf* | *f* |
| *p* | *mf* |
| *pp* | *p* |
| *ppp* | *pp* |
| | *ppp* |

The most obvious conclusion with respect to the lower dynamic
range of a piano of the Beethoven period is that it offers a positive
advantage in the soft levels and just as positive a disadvantage in the

loud levels. The dynamics of the earlier piano reveal that Beethoven was not always thundering, but that he was also deeply sensitive and reflective. He does not always speak directly to the listener, but, at times, withdraws within the privacy of his thoughts. Thus, in the opening of the third movement of Op. 110, no modern piano can produce the hushed stillness characteristic of the true *una corda* of a piano of that period. Also, due to the lower dynamic range, Alberti-bass figures need not be so carefully controlled in order not to predominate or sound busy, and the singing quality of the sound seems greater, possibly because the initial impact of the hammer is not as violent nor the tension of the string as great.

It is primarily the lack of sonority in the *forte* and *fortissimo* levels of a Beethoven-period piano which raises doubts about its suitability as a vehicle for the interpretation of Beethoven. To emphasize a caution stated earlier, one should avoid drawing conclusions such as "I like this sound, therefore Beethoven would have liked it," whether or not such would have been the case. We have grown accustomed to push-button response from the machines with which we surround ourselves, whether an automobile or a piano, and, inevitably, the more efficient the machine becomes, the more of his resourcefulness the human being discards. The confining lack of sonority in Beethoven's piano challenged the spirit of the Storm and Stress — the need to reach beyond limits and to struggle with the impossible, the acceptance of the risk that mistakes may occur and the result be failure, and the conviction that the spirit of man, which is all important, is redeemed by struggle and suffering. Writing to the publisher Steiner, Beethoven insisted that *"what is difficult is also beautiful, good, great . . ."*[25] Overcoming difficulty was a source of optimism, he reasoned in a letter to Countess Erdödy:

> Man cannot avoid suffering; and *in this respect his strength must stand the test,* that is to say, he must *endure without complaining and feel his worthlessness* and *then again* achieve *his perfection . . .*[26]

To quote Goethe in *Faust,* Part Two,

> Wer immer strebend sich bemüht,
> Den können wir erlösen!

Faced with the piano's lack of sonority, Beethoven frequently exploited the instrument's very weakness by grasping beyond its limitations. In this commentary on Op. 2/2 Tovey remarks that

pianists who have not played a Beethoven period piano cannot appreciate the effect of the *staccato fortissimi* in the A-minor section
of the Rondo. In this passage, Tovey continues, Beethóven's piano
gave the impression of producing the limit of its capacity for loudness, while the modern piano, in Tovey's opinion, sounds "weak" in
such a passage because it is capable of producing much more sound
in fuller, more brilliant writing.[27] The sense of Tovey's comment
would apply to both the examples which follow (Exx. 1,2).

Ex. 1. "Bonn" Sonata in E-flat major, WoO 47, I, 45-46

Ex. 2. Op. 111, I, 108-114

At the same time, it is absolutely necessary when playing on a
period piano to discover the level of *piano* peculiar to the instrument,
since simply matching the supposed *piano* to what one remembers
as *piano* on a modern instrument will leave no room for producing
a *forte* or a *fortissimo*. Usually one returns to a modern piano with
a heightened appreciation for its softer levels.

Because he was forced to be resourceful, Beethoven explored
other solutions to the sonority problem on his piano: sudden dynamic

changes such as a *sforzando,* a short *crescendo* or a *subito piano,* the *harmonios* pedaling to which Czerny referred so frequently and which utilized the sympathetic vibration of undamped strings, and the "sustained style," which involved the overholding and over-lapping of melody notes to produce a more convincing *legato.*

The compass of the various pianos Beethoven knew ranged from five octaves, FF through f[3], to six octaves and a fourth, CC through f[4]. Both the Erard given Beethoven by the maker in 1803[28] and the Brodmann grand which Beethoven was using at the end of his life[29] had a range of five and one-half octaves, FF through c[4]. Strangely enough, the transcription of the Violin Concerto which Beethoven made in 1807 called for a piano "with additional notes" (CC through f[4]),[30] while the Broadwood given the composer in 1818 had only six octaves, CC through c[4].[31] The fact that Broadwood had achieved this compass over 20 years earlier was indicative of his subsequent conservatism.

The compass of the Beethoven piano is not just a matter of historical interest. Hummel, in his *Piano School,* cautions against forcing the upper register of the piano to avoid hearing more wood than note.[32] This seems not to have caused Beethoven any concern, since the piano for which the *Sonata Pathétique* was written a quarter of a century earlier must have sounded even woodier at the top of the compass. In that sonata, the drama is repeatedly carried to the upper-most extremity of the usual compass of the time (Exx. 3,4).

Ex. 3. Op. 13, I, 175-187

Ex. 4. Op. 13, III, 197-202

To appreciate the sweeping gesture which this constituted on Beethoven's piano, the arrangements of Examples 5 and 6 should be tried on a modern piano.

Ex. 5.

Ex. 6.

No one would advocate that Beethoven's works be rewritten in such a fashion. However, in many instances the limited range of the treble or the bass of the piano forced Beethoven to omit the outer note of an octave or, in the case of a parallel passage in a sonata or

⁀t, to adopt a variant. In the latter situation the
⁀hould one, on a modern piano, ignore the variant
⁀ct transposition of the earlier passage? Beethoven
⁀n expected to use the higher or lower notes if these
⁀ilable; on the other hand, at times he employed a
⁀parallel passage when no compass problem was involved.
Con⁀ ⁀ what might be expected Czerny explicitly opposed any
change:

Before we take up Beethoven's compositions one by one, it is necessary to lay down a general rule.

*In the performance of his works (and in general of all classical composers) the player must throughout not permit himself any alteration of the composition, no additions, no abbreviations.*

Also, in those pieces which were written in an earlier time for the 5-octave instrument of the time, the attempt to use the 6th octave through additional notes always turns out unfavorably, just as all embellishments, mordents, trills, etc., which the composer himself has not indicated, appear superfluous, and rightly so, however tasteful these ornaments may seem in themselves. For one wants to hear the art work in its original form, as the Master conceived it and wrote it.[33]

It is safe to assume that Czerny was not referring to the addition of one missing note just beyond the compass of the earlier piano, such as the f#[3] in the first movement of Op. 10/3 (meas. 22) or the second E below the staff in the first movement of Op. 90 (meas. 214), but that he did have in mind octave doublings such as those sometimes added in the left hand to create more sound just before the recapitulation in the first movement of Op. 57, as well as the use of exact transpositions mentioned above. No doubt Czerny remembered the reproof given him by Beethoven following a performance of the Quintet, Op. 16, to the effect that he preferred hearing his works played exactly as he had written them.[34] Thus Czerny's earlier practice may not always have been in accordance with the emphatic warning given in his *Piano School*. In any event, the pianist today who avoids alterations of Beethoven's scores to exploit the range of the modern piano has the firm support of Czerny and, through him, of Beethoven himself.

Contemporary accounts of Beethoven's playing which touch

upon the durability of his piano cause one to wonder how it was possible to make music under such circumstances. On one occasion, Anton Reicha, who was turning pages for Beethoven during a performance of a Mozart concerto, related that he was kept busy removing broken strings and freeing hammers which had become entangled.[35] Another account indicates that after Beethoven had improvised for an hour at the home of Count von Dönhoff in Linz, half of the strings in the piano were broken.[36] Probably for the same reason, Beethoven, writing to Streicher in 1810, describes his Erard of 1803 as "quite useless."[37] He was equally disappointed with later pianos, on which, as he complained to Johann Stumpff, the London harp maker who visited him in 1824, it was impossible to play with "force and effect." The visitor must have had reason to agree as he gazed inside the Broadwood which had been in the composer's possession for six years. The tangle of broken strings reminded him of a "bush after a windstorm."[38]

In each instance cited above, the problem involved principally the quality of the wire used, for it was not until the introduction of the Bessemer process in 1856 that the character of steel could be controlled with certainty.[39] It may be impossible, in this technically pampered age, to decide whether Beethoven appeared frustrated by his structurally inadequate piano, or whether his playing seemed more awesome because the instrument was incapable of producing the demands he placed upon it.

**Beethoven's Improvisation.** — The average listener of Beethoven's time was more curious to hear new works by new composers than is his counterpart today. One reason for this may be that improvisation, except in the area of jazz, is no longer cultivated by pianists. When musical training concentrates upon the "how" of performance, competition produces a high technical quality in such performance while improvisation places the individual in the midst of the composer's problems.

The emphasis upon the external side of performance was already developing in Beethoven's lifetime, concurrently, it might be added, with the coming of age of the piano. Beethoven was aware of the difference in performing attitude and spoke of it during a conversation with Tomaschek in the year 1814:

It has always been known that the greatest pianoforte players were also the greatest composers; but how did they play?

> Not like the pianists of today, who prance up and down the
> keyboard with passages which they have practised — *putsch,
> putsch, putsch;* — what does that mean? Nothing! When true
> pianoforte virtuosi played it was always something homo-
> geneous, an entity; if written down it would appear as a well
> thought-out work. That is pianoforte playing; the other
> thing is nothing![40]

Reading Beethoven's comment gives today's pianist the uncomfortable feeling of being personally indicted. Beethoven probably did
as much improvisation in public as performances of his completed
works. Ries indicates that:

> He played his own compositions very unwillingly. Once he
> was making serious preparations for a long trip which we
> were to make together, on which I was to arrange the con-
> certs and play his concertos as well as other compositions.
> He himself wanted to conduct and only to improvise.[41]

On the subject of the performance of completed works, Ries relates
that Beethoven played very whimsically, and Czerny adds that, because of his facility in improvising, he had no patience for practice.[42]
    A key to understanding one facet of Beethoven's ability to im-
provise is found in the connection between chord fingering and the
realization of figured bass as it is presented by Philipp Emanuel Bach
in his *Essay on the True Art of Playing Keyboard Instruments.* According to his own statement, Bach and his father were diametrically
opposed to Rameau's principles.[43] Rather than approach improvisation from the standpoint of a theoretical fundamental bass and chord
classification based on root movement, Bach's method of studying
chords, as William Mitchell, the translator and editor of the modern
edition of the *Essay,* explains, was to develop first the tactile sense of
associating an appropriate fingering with a figured bass symbol. In
the *Essay,* chords are presented according to the figured bass interval
forming their outside parts — triads, chords of the sixth, six-four-
three, six-five, six-four-two, chords of the seventh, etc.[44] Thus, a
broken pattern of any chord is played with the same fingering previously established for the intervals comprising that chord. Beethoven's facility with this tactile approach to the realization of figured
bass and improvisation was the basis for the ruse used by visitors
who, in Beethoven's later years, wanted to hear him play. A request
was sure to be turned down, but if one pretended to find something

wrong with a particular note on the piano, Beethoven would become interested — trying the note, adding a fifth, then another interval — all of which then led to the desired improvisation.[45]

Czerny used the word *preludiren* to describe the use of figuration in beginning an improvisation. From this commonplace raw material the improviser would fashion themes which he then developed. To appreciate this approach to improvisation, it is well worth noting that Beethoven's activity with technical exercises is almost totally confined to his sketchbooks. To rephrase a remark of Czerny, Beethoven had no time for exercises which were divorced from musical purpose.[46] Although a few of the exercises given here, which are reproduced in Nottebohm's *Zweite Beethoveniana,* scarcely appear to be exercises, each illustrates Beethoven's manner of searching out the musical possibilities inherent in improvisatory material of the *preludiren* type (Exx. 7-22). In a few cases it is also possible to discern similarities in passages from completed works. All explanatory comments accompanying the examples are by Beethoven.

Ex. 7.

Ex. 8. Op. 110, III, 131-136

Ex. 9.

finally as soft as possible

Ex. 10. Op. 58, II, 61

Ex. 11.

The held notes in the bass produce a good effect because the bass lasts longer than such notes in a high register.

Ex. 12. Op. 106, IV, 9-10

Ex. 13.

Ex. 14. Op. 2/3, IV, 273-279

Ex. 15.

(Right Hand)

Ex. 16. Op. 53, III, 62-66

Ex. 17. Op. 2/3, I, 243-245

Ex. 18.

Op. 2/2, IV, 100-101

Ex. 20. (For practicing the fist.)

Ex. 21. Op. 2/2, I, 1-4

Ex. 22. Op. 31/3, II, 90-92

Many Beethoven themes indicate an origin in an improvisatory mutation of a triad. In the first movement of Op. 31/2 one has the impression of being present when the theme was being discovered, for the D-minor motive with which the movement seems to begin (meas. 21) appears in latent form in the rolled A-major sixth chord at the beginning. Here character is the sole interest-sustaining element. In fact, one might go so far as to say that it was principally the quality of character — or "effect" (referring to the listener's psychological response to Beethoven's playing) — which sustained the life of Beethoven's improvisations. Schenk, with whom Beethoven secretly studied counterpoint at the same time that he was studying with Haydn, described his improvisations as "psychological pictures."[47] On the occasion of the first encounter with Steibelt, Beethoven could not be induced to improvise after Steibelt had played since the latter had produced a stunning effect with his use of tremolos, which, at that time, were still a novelty.[48] The experience of hearing Beethoven improvise was not easily forgotten. The effect was still a vivid memory when Czerny wrote the following description in 1852, a quarter of a century after Beethoven's death.

> His improvisation was most brilliant and striking. In whatever company he might chance to be, he knew how to produce such an effect upon every hearer that frequently not an eye remained dry, while many would break out into loud sobs; for there was something wonderful in his expression in addition to the beauty and originality of his ideas and his spirited style of rendering them.[49]

Czerny's vocabulary of character-words to describe the effect Beethoven's works should have if played correctly is extensive. The following list, taken from the *Piano School,* is by no means complete, yet it gives an idea of the richness of this "interpretive vocabulary."

| | | | |
|---|---|---|---|
| unruly | serious | tragic | teasing |
| weighty | fantastic | humorous | pathetic |
| lulling | firm | intimate | bewitching |
| determined | fleeting | complaining | religious |
| brilliant | joyous | strong | roaring |
| singing | pious | noisy | peaceful |
| capriciously | tender | lively | touching |
| chorale-like | witty | light | gentle |
| delicate | good-natured | charming | jocose |
| dramatic | powerful | virile | flattering |
| exalted | sparkling | marked | dejected |
| simple | expressively | melancholy | speaking |
| elegant | graceful | merry | stormy |
| mournful | shrill | murmuring | agitated |
| energetic | grand | mischievous | profound |
| resolute | serene | naive | dreamy |
| lofty | heroic | unaffected | sensitive |

The significance of the great variety of these interpretive indications is that Czerny was describing character as he knew it from Beethoven's playing and teaching. The mere presence of this extensive vocabulary reflects the importance of character delineation in Beethoven's playing, including, of course, his improvisation. One might also attach some importance to those particular words Czerny used more frequently than others: *ernst, kräftig, ausdrucksvoll, sanft, gefühlsvoll, zart, lebhaft, leicht, ruhig, markirt, brillant, cantabile.*

If Beethoven's improvisation was convincing, it was in large measure due to his rhetorical manner of playing. In terms of musical interpretation, a rhetorical manner means the use of pauses, produced either by a rest or a *fermata,* to separate sections of differing character. On the first page of Beethoven's *Fantasie, Op. 77,* which may be regarded as a written improvisation, there are seven such pauses, separating passages of alternating slow and fast tempos, as well as of scale and cantabile writing. If one did not object to these abrupt changes of direction, the rhetorical pause was ideally suited to heighten the character of a section so set off. Along with the stress upon character over learned devices, the use of rhetorical pauses to separate important ideas helps to explain Beethoven's reputed ability to repeat an improvisation intact.[50]

Baroness Dorothea von Ertmann, Archduke Rudolph of Austria, Karl Czerny, Ferdinand Ries, Ignaz Moscheles, Anton Schindler — these are the more important of that group of persons privileged to call themselves students of Beethoven. They were a divergent group: amateurs and professionals, royalty and commoners, congenial and egotistical, teachers and concertizing pianists, prolific writers and the historically silent.

The principal sources for the purpose of this study will be Czerny and Schindler, two men who were very different personally. Unassuming, industrious and precocious, Czerny was an unusually gifted pianist. Like young Moscheles, Czerny became an ardent Beethoven enthusiast while yet a child. Through contact with Wenzel Krumpholz, a violinist in the Vienna opera orchestra and one of Beethoven's earliest and most loyal champions, Czerny was kept informed of the progress of ·Beethoven's newest work as well as his wishes regarding the way it should be played. Czerny, with his unusual capability for memorization, learned these works as they appeared. When he was ten years old, Krumpholz introduced him to Beethoven.[51]

Czerny's first impression was that Beethoven's appearance reminded him of Robinson Crusoe. He noticed the medicated cotton which Beethoven had in his ears, the appearance of his hands — "overgrown with hair," and the shape of his fingers —"very broad" at the tips. Not wishing to begin with one of Beethoven's own compositions, Czerny played first the Mozart C-major Concerto, K. 503, for which Beethoven played parts of the orchestral *tutti* with his left hand in the treble of the piano. Since Beethoven seemed satisfied, Czerny felt confident enough to play the *Sonata Pathétique,* which had been published in the fall of 1799. As a result, Czerny was accepted by Beethoven as a student and, for a time, received lessons twice weekly.[52]

Czerny's account of his first lessons with Beethoven indicates that the first project consisted of scales in all keys through which Beethoven taught him the correct position of the hands and fingers, and, above all, the use of the thumb, practices which, according to Czerny, were unknown to most players of the time. Thereafter, Beethoven proceeded to the practice pieces belonging to the Bach *Essay,* followed by his own variations on a theme from Süssmayer's *Soliman* and, after this, the Sonata, Op. 13.[53] Czerny also studied with Beethoven the Sonatas, Op. 14, 31/2, 101, and the *Andante* of Op. 28, all the concertos (with the exception of Op. 19), the Choral Fantasy, and the "Archduke" Trio. In addition, he is known to have read the Sonata, Op. 53, before Beethoven from the manuscript and to have played Op. 57 for the composer on several occasions. It is likely also that Czerny studied Op. 106 with Beethoven prior to his performance of it on the series of Sunday concerts devoted to works of Beethoven in his home during the winters of 1818 to 1820.[54]

Czerny's boyish awe of Beethoven did not stifle his healthy curiosity about other musicians. Among these was Hummel, whose clarity of performance impressed him greatly. Although Czerny did not tour Europe or have a career as a concertizing pianist, as did Ries, Moscheles, and Kalkbrenner, he did play, both in private and in public. During one season he played as often as twice a week for Prince Lichnowsky — the Prince had only to indicate the opus number, and Czerny played the work by memory.[55] He was also soloist in both the C-major Concerto (1806) and the E-flat Concerto (1812) of Beethoven, although he had to refuse Beethoven's request to play the E-flat Concerto in 1818, since, as he explained, his teaching occupied twelve hours a day, leaving him no time for practice. Czerny was thus akin both to the Beethoven following and the world of the virtuoso and yet, seemingly, not completely successful in either. Frimmel states that "in Beethoven's circle, Czerny's playing was already thought extravagant."[56] Schindler, for example, traced the flamboyant movements which he found objectionable in Liszt's playing directly back to Czerny's teaching.[57]

By far the most prolific writer of any of Beethoven's students, Anton Felix Schindler met Beethoven in March 1814 as a youth of eighteen. The circumstance leading to the meeting — a request to deliver a message to Beethoven — was as unplanned as it was prophetic, for within five years Schindler became Beethoven's unpaid secretary and servant. As a human being he was utterly devoted to Beethoven, who, as often as not, rewarded this devotion with contempt and abuse. Nevertheless, Schindler remained a staunch defender of his teacher and a self-appointed spiritual caretaker of Beethoven's works after his death. Although he was primarily a violinist and an excellent one — fine enough to become concertmaster of the orchestra in the Josephstadt Theater — his biographer Hueffer recorded that Schindler played the piano often for Beethoven during the years 1818 to 1821 and that, on these occasions, Beethoven would then play for him, explaining the interpretation of the particular movement or sonata.[58] For this reason, Donald MacArdle came to the conclusion that Schindler may have been more intimately acquainted with Beethoven's wishes than any other individual.[59] Moreover, in one important respect both Schindler and Beethoven (at least during the years Schindler was closely associated with him) thought alike — neither was interested in piano playing in and for itself. Since Schindler's style at times seems vague and misleading, it is fortunate that he singled out the biography of Beethoven by Adolf Bernhard Marx, *Beethoven, Leben und Schaffen,* as being closely allied to his own views.[60]

Partly due to the fact that he was not primarily a pianist, and partly to the derision he was accorded, Schindler took out his bitterness on the virtuosi of the day, who were also the successful performers continually before the public. He had no admiration for Ries, Moscheles, Mendelssohn, and Clara Schumann. Considering that he was not an inarticulate man when attacking shallowness in others by his standards, he had no difficulty making enemies. The response of those who had been stung by Schindler's criticisms is shown in the following entry in Moscheles' diary:

> . . . His egotism is the chief feature throughout; it is *"I"* perpetually; "Clementi, Cramer, Beethoven and *I*" worked together for the promotion and welfare of art. "Hummel and Moscheles have perverted pianoforte-playing. The latter (says he) has actually had the audacity to set to metronome Tempi works of Beethoven, *whom he never heard play"* . . . Ferdinand Hiller published a letter to Schindler in reply . . . and asked him, "if he has ever got so far in his whole life, as to be able to play Cramer's first Study? Can he show him a single trace anywhere of any one composition by Schindler? or has he, as a conductor, a past history only known to himself?". . . Hiller concludes with Goethe's words, " 'None but good-for-nothings are modest,' therefore pray discard all modesty, and enlighten on the subject your, as far as possible, humble servant . . ."[61]

It is unfortunate that Schindler's defensive and vindictive nature obscured the validity of his views. His "feel" for Beethoven's intentions was sufficiently sound; he did not need to distort facts or attitudes to defend his beliefs. Moscheles, following his introduction to Beethoven in 1809, *had* taken advantage of every opportunity to see and hear the composer. He attended the Schuppanzigh quartet performances, at which Beethoven was often present, and the Augarten concerts, in which he appeared as director and on occasion as pianist. Beyond this, he came in contact with Beethoven privately at the homes of wealthy admirers, where he was impressed by the audacity of amateur pianists in playing Beethoven's works before the composer himself.[62] It was not until 1814, during the time when Moscheles was preparing the piano score of *Fidelio,* that the two men developed a personal friendship.

After Beethoven's death, the complete piano sonatas were published twice under Moscheles' editorship, once in 1838-1839 by Cramer and again in 1858 by Hallberger in Leipzig. Moscheles' contribution to the edition consisted of metronome markings, additional dynamic markings, phrasing and pedaling. He was guided, he claimed, not by his musical instinct alone, but by his recollections of Beethoven's playing and that of his student, the Baroness Ertmann.

. . . I hope in this new publication to be permitted to complete, with traditional correctness, many a gap in the signs of interpretation which Beethoven *played* but did not write down, and which every intelligent musician can add, but which is intended to make the finest nuances clear to the amateur.[63]

The Baroness was a student of Beethoven for many years, beginning in 1803, and, until her husband's transfer to Milan in 1818, one of Beethoven's finest interpreters. In spite of the fact that she played only privately, Schindler believed that if it had not been for her performances Beethoven's works would have disappeared from the repertoire far earlier than they actually did.[64] Schindler described her sense for "free tempo" as instinctive, adding that no one had reproduced Beethoven's own manner of playing as closely as she.[65] The Baroness was held in equally high esteem by Czerny, Clementi and Moscheles.

Remembering Schindler's lack of admiration for Mendelssohn as a virtuoso pianist, it is interesting to read Mendelssohn's description of performance by the Baroness. Beethoven's dedication of the Sonata, Op. 101, to her was common knowledge in musical circles of the time. Mendelssohn, in 1831, while passing through Milan and hearing the name Ertmann, immediately made the association in his mind and decided to pay a visit. She played for him the C-sharp minor Sonata, Op. 27, and the D-minor Sonata, Op. 31. According to Kalischer, the General "wept for joy" to hear his wife play once more, because "there is no one in Milan who wants to listen to something like this." Mendelssohn wrote his sister:

> She plays the Beethoven things beautifully, although she has not studied for a long time, often exaggerates the expression a little and holds back a great deal and then hurries again; however, she plays single pieces gloriously, and I believe I have learned something from her.[66]

# Notes and Sources

## Chapter I

[1]*Thayer's Life of Beethoven,* revised and edited by Elliot Forbes (Princeton: Princeton University Press, 1967; Princeton Paperback, 1970), Vol. I, p. 79.

[2]Ludwig Schiedermair, *Der Junge Beethoven* (Leipzig: Quelle & Meyer, 1925), p. 158.

[3]*Ibid.,* p. 73.

[4]*Ibid.,* p. 78.

[5]*Ibid.,* p. 154.

[6]Gerhard von Breuning, *Aus dem Schwarzspanierhause* (Vienna, 1874), p. 9.

[7]Ernst Cassirer, *The Question of Jean-Jacques Rousseau* (Bloomington: Indiana University Press, 1963), p. 83.

[8]Roy Pascal, *The German Sturm und Drang* (New York: Philosophical Library, 1953), p. 145.

[9]Franz Gerhard Wegeler and Ferdinand Ries, *Biographische Notizen über Ludwig van Beethoven* (Coblenz, 1838), pp. 94-95.

[10]Anton Schindler, *Beethoven as I Knew Him,* edited by Donald W. MacArdle (Chapel Hill: The University of North Carolina Press, 1966), p. 413.

[11]Edward Bellasis, *Cherubini: Memorials Illustrative of His Life* (London, 1874), p. 160.

[12]Pascal, p. 22.

[13]Carl Czerny, *Vollständige theoretisch-practische Pianoforte-Schule, Op. 500* (Vienna, 1842), Vol. IV, p. 34.

[14]Schindler, p. 413.

[15]Carl Philipp Emanuel Bach, *Essay on the True Art of Playing Keyboard Instruments,* translated and edited by William J. Mitchell (New York: W. W. Norton & Company, 1949), p. 152.

[16]Pascal, p. 275.

[17]Schindler, p. 406.

[18]Czerny, *Pianoforte-Schule,* Vol. IV, p. 51.

[19]*Ibid.,* p. 56.

[20]*Ibid.,* p. 62.

[21]Schindler, p. 424.

[22]*Ibid.,* p. 400.

[23]*Ibid.,* p. 139.

[24]*Poems of Goethe,* edited by Ronald Gray (Cambridge: University Press, 1966), p. 156.

[25]Emily Anderson, *The Letters of Beethoven* (New York: St. Martin's Press, 1961; London: Macmillan & Co.), Vol. II, p. 661.

[26]*Ibid.,* p. 578

[27]Donald Francis Tovey and Harold Craxton (ed.), *Beethoven Sonatas* (London: Associated Board of the Royal Schools of Music, 1931), Vol. I, p. 32.

[28]Schindler, p. 191.

[29]Breuning, p. 24.

[30]Schindler, p. 193.

[31]Thayer-Forbes, Vol. II, p. 694.

[32]Johann Nepomuk Hummel, *A Complete Theoretical and Practical Course of Instruction in the Art of Playing the Piano Forte* (London, 1827), p. 42.

[33]Czerny, *Pianoforte-Schule,* Vol. IV, p. 34.

[34]Anderson, Vol. II, p. 560.

[35]Harold Schonberg, *The Great Pianists* (New York: Simon and Schuster, 1963), p. 74.

[36]Thayer-Forbes, Vol. I, p. 541.

[37]Anderson, Vol. I, p. 292.

[38]Ernest Closson, *History of the Piano* (London: Paul Elek, 1947), pp. 100-101.

[39]*Encyclopaedia Britannica* (Chicago: William Benton, 1958), Vol. 3, p. 474.

[40]Thayer-Forbes, Vol. I, p. 599.

[41]Wegeler and Ries, p. 100.

[42]Thayer-Forbes, Vol. I, pp. 368-369.

[43]Bach, *Essay,* p. 17.

[44]*Ibid.,* pp. 17-18.

[45]Theodor von Frimmel, *Beethoven Studien* (Munich and Leipzig, 1904-1906).

[46]Schindler, p. 413.

[47]Thayer-Forbes, Vol. I, p. 140.

[48]*Ibid.,* p. 257.

[49]*Ibid.,* p. 185.

[50]*Ibid.,* p. 224.

[51]*Ibid.,* pp. 226-227.

[52]Carl Czerny, *Ueber den richtigen Vortag der Sämtlichen Bee-thoven'schen Klavierwerke* (Vienna: Universal Edition, 1963), pp. 10-11.

[53]Czerny, *Pianoforte-Schule,* Vol. IV, p. 74.

[54]Czerny, *Ueber den richtigen Vortrag,* p. 9.

[55]Anna Gertrud Huber, *Ludwig van Beethoven, Seine Schüler und Interpreten* (Vienna: Walter Krieg, 1953), p. 20.

[56]Schindler, p. 449.

[57]*Ibid.,* p. 416.

[58]*Ibid.,* p. 446.

[59]*Ibid.,* p. 446.

[60]*Ibid.,* p. 29.

[61]Charlotte Moscheles, *Life of Moscheles* (London, 1873), p. 144.

[62]Alfred Christian Kalischer, *Beethoven und seine Zeitgenossen* (Berlin and Leipzig: Schuster & Loeffler, 1909-1910), Vol. IV, p. 46.

[63]Ignaz Moscheles (ed.), *Beethoven Sonatas* (Leipzig: Hallberger, 1858), preface.

[64]Kalischer, Vol. III, p. 116.

[65]Schindler, p. 210.

[66]Kalischer, Vol. III, pp. 121-123.

# II

# Tempo and
# Modifications of Tempo

IN SCHINDLER'S *Beethoven as I Knew Him,* one reads:

> When a work of Beethoven had been performed, his first question was always, "How were the tempi?" Every other consideration seemed to be of secondary importance to him.[1]

The following passages from the Czerny *Piano School* support Schindler's statement:

> These variations [Op. 34] require a performance which is as adroit and finished as it is sensitive, and the character of each is so clearly delineated that the player cannot miss it if he chooses the correct tempo.[2]

> . . . . . . . . . . . . . . . . . . . . . . . . . . . . . . . . . . . . . . . . .

> There are substantial considerations, which are absolutely necessary and upon which everything else depends, namely:

> First, the right tempo.

> . . . . . . . . . . . . . . . . . . . . . . . . . . . . . . . . . . . . . . . . .

> We have attempted throughout to indicate the most appropriate tempo by means of the Maelzel metronome as well as by means of words, and the observance of this is to be sure the most important, since the whole character of the piece will be distorted by a false tempo.[3]

To play a piece according to a given metronome marking, even if the marking has been supplied by Czerny, does not settle the matter of tempo. Similarly, Beethoven was uncertain whether tempo indications, even his own metronome markings, could indicate the tempo at which a piece should be played. In a letter written in 1817, he states that he would just as soon dispense with the traditional indications (*Presto, Allegro, Andante,* etc.) and in place of these use words and phrases describing the character of the work. A traditional tempo marking, in Beethoven's opinion, was to be likened to the body, while a character indication was analogous to the spirit.[4]

Since character may be defined as the quality which the response of the listener ascribes to the piece as meaning, both Beethoven and Czerny were indicating that the right tempo is the one which sustains psychological response. In a sense this is true of all music — the success of the work depends upon whether it sustains interest. In Beethoven the interrelationship between tempo and psychological response is much more highly charged due to the fact that length and content frequently produce an opposite effect, or at least introduce an unsettling element, as anti-interest-sustaining agents.

In *Beethoven as I Knew Him* Schindler quotes a brief review of the "Emperor" Concerto from the *Allgemeine Musikalische Zeitung* which complained that the impact of the work was weakened by its length. At the time of his writing, Schindler doubted that anyone would find the Concerto long, adding that it was originally this sort of external consideration which occasioned the greatest objection to Beethoven's works.[5] This may also have been the reason why Czerny cautions against revealing all the power of the finale of the "Appassionata" at once. With its long repeat of the second half, the movement "should be only rarely stormy," picking up tempo and strength "first with the repeat of the second half" and continuing then into the close.[6]

Besides length, content caused the listener and performer of Beethoven's day to question whether his music was really worth the effort. If the work did not strike one as sounding pretty or feeling grateful to the fingers, the natural human reaction was to lay it aside as something contrived, unmelodious, artificial, empty and exhausting to player and listener alike. In the passage from the "Archduke" Trio quoted below, the player has two alternatives, play the figure between the hands or play it with the right hand alone (Ex. 23). The passage will not sound brilliant, even if divided between the hands, because it is not that kind of writing. As for the second alternative, the few notes which are there are so inconveniently arranged that one's accuracy when striving to play *fortissimo* is compromised. One answer, which to this writer seems the only one, is that this is a point where music ceases to be music

and becomes realism, in this case the realism of the human experience of struggle. In the best Storm and Stress sense art is linked
with personal experience, and only the right tempo — a driving

Ex. 23. Op. 97, I, 104-106

tempo — can bring it off. Representative of a procedure, rather
than isolated instances, Examples 24-26 share a peculiar similarity
with respect to content. Each is constructed of an extended repetition of a pattern with little or no dynamic change, although, in a
few of the examples, the pace quickens as the pattern is shortened
near the close of the section. Because the individual examples are
lengthy, only the beginning and ending of each is given. In character,

Ex. 24. Op. 22, I, 91-104

Ex. 25. Op. 31/2, III, 110-150

Ex. 26. Op. 53, I, 112-137

all the passages given above seem more intensely goal-directed than in sight of a goal. The music is "about" driving energy, the force of which will never be felt if a safe, comfortable tempo is chosen since such a tempo betrays the repetitive nature of the writing. Long passages of sameness on a *piano* level, as in the fourth variation of the Arietta of Op. 111, have a peaceful character which avoids all semblance of external activity (Ex. 27). To maintain this desirable quality of suspended motion, it is as important not to rush the tempo as it was not to permit the tempo to "plod" in the passages shown in examples 24-26.

Ex. 27. Op. 111, II, Variation 4

Before the widespread distribution of the metronome, Czerny suggested that performances in which Mozart or Beethoven played or conducted could have been timed, so that posterity might have had some idea of the tempi chosen by the composer.

If at that time . . . someone had come upon the simple idea of timing the duration of every movement and then making note of it exactly in minutes and seconds, we would now have the most reliable measure of how fast every piece is supposed to be played, according to the intention of the composer. Why should that not be possible from now on? Unfortunately one cannot always count on everyone having a metronome. But if a player knows, for example, that a piece has to take exactly 8½ minutes, he will discover by the second or at most the third playing how fast or how slowly he must take the tempo in order to fill out the time exactly. So also the orchestra conductor. And since clocks have the same unchanging pace constantly and everywhere, and always will have, such an indication, given by the composer himself, would remain understandable to the last generation. By giving this idea cursory mention here, we believe we may have perhaps stimulated the adoption and refinement of this idea. It is known how frequently, especially in public performances, the tempo is misjudged. It goes without saying that, in larger works, there would be a variation of a few moments, since the nature of the hall, of the orchestra, etc., has to allow for a small difference.[7]

A study of a series of timings made by Sir George Smart during the years 1819 through 1843 has been made by Nicholas Temperley of the University of Illinois. As simple as the idea appeared to Czerny, accurate comparisons between these timings and timings of performances of the same works today are very difficult to make. As Temperley indicates, one does not know which, if any, repeats were made, what cuts may have been used and the extent of these cuts, how much time was taken between movements, the length of cadenzas, and of course the possibility for error on the part of the person doing the timing.[8]

Experiments with chronometers had been made prior to the perfection of the Maelzel metronome. A primitive type consisted of a lead weight either suspended on a string with knots marking the points which would produce oscillations of the desired speed or instead suspended on a rod, like a clock pendulum. If justice had been done, the metronome today would be known as Winkel's Metronome, after Dietrich Nikolaus Winkel, a Dutch mechanician whose invention of a double pendulum solved the problem of the great length of pendulum needed for a slow tempo. Maelzel, who saw Winkel's chronometer after it had been described and commended by the Dutch Academy of Sciences in 1815, tried unsuccessfully to purchase rights to the invention from Winkel. Consequently, Maelzel adapted the idea of the double pendulum to a metronome of his own, added a graduated scale (his only contribution to Winkel's machine), and acquired a patent for the "Maelzel Metronome" in London and Paris. When Winkel became aware of what had happened he brought the matter before the Dutch Academy of Sciences. Although this body decided in Winkel's favor, it was already too late, since the association in the popular mind between the name of Maelzel and the invention had already become too strong to change.[9]

Of the sonatas, Beethoven provided metronome markings only for Op. 106:

| | | |
|---|---|---|
| Allegro | $\half$ | = 138 |
| Scherzo: Assai vivace | $\dotquarter$ | = 80 |
| Adagio sostenuto | $\eighth$ | = 92 |

Largo                    ♪ = 76
Allegro risoluto         ♩ = 144

Since Czerny worked with Beethoven in the preparation of this sonata for performance on his house concert series, his comments on the sonata and its metronome markings are significantly instructive. In the *Piano School,* he refers to the "uncommonly quick and fiery tempo" indicated by Beethoven as the chief difficulty in playing the first movement. Furthermore, he does not say that he played it less fast — one's conception of the orchestrally conceived first movement develops with frequent playing, "after one has already learned it correctly in the proper tempo."[10] Moscheles thought the Beethoven marking impossible and suggested as a tempo for the first movement ♩ = 116.

Schindler adds to the uncertainty surrounding the selection of appropriate metronome markings by maintaining that Maelzel had a smaller, less expensive metronome made in Vienna for his German customers. If Schindler's information is reliable, the pendulum rod of Maelzel's Viennese metronome was provided with a wider range of numbers than was the larger Maelzel metronome made in Paris. The markings which Beethoven made for all the symphonies were supposedly done with the smaller metronome and, consequently, would be useless if reproduced on the larger model on which, following Schindler's reasoning, the same number gave a slower beat.[11] Nottebohm denies this, stating that all Maelzel metronomes were built according to the same system, based upon the division of the minute: "If it beats more or less often, it is out of order, or it is no Maelzel Metronome."[12] One would like to believe that the alleged difference in scale between the two metronomes was merely the result of confusion on Schindler's part. However, doubts arise again when Czerny's statement on his metronome markings for the Sonatas is taken into consideration: "In setting these markings we have used the V i e n n a — Metronome."[13] Neither does it increase one's confidence to read of the experience of Sir George Smart testing twelve metronomes and finding that none beat together.[14]

Machines are imperfect, and minds are subject to change. Schindler tells of helping Beethoven set the metronome markings for the Ninth Symphony, which were to be sent to the Philharmonic Society in London. After they had established the markings, a set for the same work, made a few days earlier for Mainz, turned up in the disorder of Beethoven's apartment. To the composer's dismay, a comparison of the two versions revealed a discrepancy in all movements. Beethoven's reaction was to declare metronome markings useless — unnecessary for perceptive musicians and meaningless for the unmusical, for whom nothing would help.[15] However, in December 1826 Beethoven wrote to the publisher Schott in Mainz, requesting that he wait for the metronome markings for a quartet; he was convinced, he wrote, that the success of the Ninth Symphony in Berlin was to be attributed in large part to the observance of the metronome markings.[16]

The table which follows compares the metronome markings for the Sonatas as indicated by Czerny in the *Piano School* (1842) and the Simrock Edition of 1850, by Moscheles in the Hallberger Edition (1858), and, to provide perspective, by the editors of two editions widely used during the past fifty years — Bülow and Schnabel.

In support of his choice of metronome markings, Czerny recalls his house concerts, begun in 1816 and devoted chiefly to works of Beethoven, in preparation for which Beethoven had indicated the tempi. (Thayer disputes Czerny's claim that Beethoven was "almost always" present at these concerts.) Czerny says of his study with Beethoven: "On the whole, Beethoven was satisfied with my performance of his works; however, he corrected every mistake with charitable frankness, which I will never forget."[17] Nottebohm also had high regard for Czerny:

> Whoever knew Czerny personally, whoever had an opportunity to observe above all his practical nature believed in his capacity to impress upon his memory a tempo that had been heard. . . .[18]

In making the metronome markings for the Simrock edition, Czerny did not simply copy those made eight years earlier but instead restudied all of them. Those sonatas or individual movements in the table below which Czerny indicated he had studied with Beethoven are marked with an asterisk.

Moscheles, like Czerny, had known Beethoven, heard him play and listened to performances of the composer's works in his presence. In setting metronome markings for some of the fast movements, he declared that he had deliberately tried to avoid the virtuosic inclination of the day; his metronome markings in general, he maintained, differed only slightly from those of Czerny, whose competence he respected.[19] The metronome markings of Moscheles given below also represent a revision of those given in an earlier edition which he had done for Cramer and Company in England in 1838-1839.

| | | Czerny 1842 | Czerny 1850 | Moscheles | Bülow | Schnabel |
|---|---|---|---|---|---|---|
| **Op. 2/1** | | | | | | |
| Allegro | ♩ = 104 | | 108 | 108 | 112 | 126-138 |
| Adagio | ♪ = 80 | | 84 | 100[20] | 88 | 88 |
| Allegretto | ♩. = 69 | | 72 | 72 | 63 | 58 |
| Prestissimo | ♩ = 104 | | 108 | 112 | 104 | 116 |
| **Op. 2/2** | | | | | | |
| Allegro vivace | ♩ = 132 | | 138 | 144 | 132 | 152 |
| Largo appassionato | ♪ = 80 | | 88 | 88 | 76 | 69 |
| Allegretto | ♩. = 63 | | 66 | 60 | 58 | 56 |
| Grazioso | ♩ = 132 | | 144 | 144 | 112 | 132 |
| **Op. 2/3** | | | | | | |
| Allegro con brio | ♩ = 80 | | 80 | 76 | 72[21] | 76[22] |
| Adagio | ♪ = 50 | | 56 | 56 | 54 | 46 |
| Allegro | ♩. = 80 | | 76 | 88 | 76 | 104 |
| Allegro assai | ♪. = 116 | | 116 | 116 | 112 | 126 |
| **Op. 7** | | | | | | |
| Allegro molto e con brio | ♪. = 116 | | 126 | 126 | 126 | 132 |
| Largo con gran espressione | ♪ = 80 | | 84 | 100[23] | 92 | 72-80 |
| Allegro | ♩. = 72 | | 80 | 80 | 76 | 69 |
| Poco Allegretto | ♩ = 60 | | 66[24] | 69[25] | 60 | 69 |
| **Op. 10/1** | | | | | | |
| Allegro molto e con brio | ♩. = 72 | | 76 | 76 | 69 | 76-88 |
| Adagio molto | ♪ = 69 | | 72 | 72 | 69 | 63 |
| Prestissimo | ♩ = 96 | | 100 | 108 | 100 | 104-112 |

| | | Czerny 1842 | Czerny 1850 | Moscheles | Bülow | Schnabel |
|---|---|---|---|---|---|---|
| **Op. 10/2** | | | | | | |
| Allegro | ♩ = | 104 | 108 | 112 | 108 | 104 |
| Allegretto | ♩. = | 72 | 76 | 72 | 69 | 66 |
| Presto | ♩ = | 80 | 80[26] | 80[27] | 84 | 84-92 |
| **Op. 10/3** | | | | | | |
| Presto | ♩ = | 126 | 132 | 132 | 132 | 152-168 |
| Largo e mesto | ♪ = | 72 | 76 | 72 | 56 | 63 |
| Allegro | ♩. = | 76 | 84 | 84 | 69 | 92-100 |
| Allegro | ♩ = | 152 | 152 | 152 | 126 | 144 |
| ***Op. 13** | | | | | | |
| Grave | ♪ = | 46[28] | 63 | 60 | 66 | 52 |
| Allegro molto e con brio | ♩ = | 144 | 144 | 144 | 144 | 168-176 |
| Adagio cantabile | ♪ = | 54 | 60 | 60 | 60 | 60 |
| Allegro | ♩ = | 96 | 104 | 104 | 96 | 108 |
| ***Op. 14/1** | | | | | | |
| Allegro | ♩ = | 132 | 144 | 152 | 138 | 126 |
| Allegretto | ♩. = | 69 | 72 | 72 | 60 | 50 |
| Allegro commodo | ♩ = | | 96 | 80[29] | 76 | 80 |
| ***Op. 14/2** | | | | | | |
| Allegro | ♩ = | 80 | 80[30] | 80[31] | 84 | 104 |
| Andante | ♩ = | 116 | 112 | 96 | 76 | 72 |
| Allegro assai | ♩. = | 80 | 88 | 88 | 76 | 88 |
| **Op. 22** | | | | | | |
| Allegro con brio | ♩ = | 76 | 84 | 84 | 69[32] | 80-84[33] |
| Adagio con molto espressione | ♪ = | 100 | 116 | 116 | 100 | 84 |
| Menuetto | ♩ = | 120 | 126 | 126 | 104 | 100 |
| Allegretto | ♩ = | 69 | 76 | 76 | 63 | 80-84 |

| | | Czerny 1842 | 1850 | Moscheles | Bülow | Schnabel |
|---|---|---|---|---|---|---|
| **Op. 26** | | | | | | |
| Andante | | | | | | |
| (Theme) | ♪ = | 76 | 80 | 80 | 80 | 63-66 |
| Variation 1 | ♪ = | | 88 | 88 | 88 | |
| Variation 2 | ♪ = | 92 | 100 | 104 | 96 | 88 |
| Variation 3 | ♪ = | 76 | 92 | 92 | 80 | 63-66 |
| Variation 4 | ♪ = | 92 | 100 | 100 | 92 | 84 |
| Variation 5 | ♪ = | 76 | 80 | 80 | 88 | 63-66 |
| Allegro molto | ♩. = | 92 | 88 | 88 | 88 | 112 |
| Marcia funebre | ♩ = | 72 | 66 | 60 | 72 | 52 |
| Allegro | ♩ = | 132 | 120 | 108 | 116 | 160 |
| **Op. 27/1** | | | | | | |
| Andante | ♩ = | 66 | 69 | 76 | 84 | 72 |
| Allegro | ♩. = | 104 | 104 | 104 | 84 | 108 |
| Allegro molto | | | | | | |
| vivace | •♩. = | 112 | 120 | 126 | 100 | 132 |
| Adagio con | | | | | | |
| espressione | ♪ = | 66 | 72 | 76 | 66 | 63 |
| Allegro vivace | ♩ = | 132 | 132 | 120 | 126 | 138 |
| **Op. 27/2** | | | | | | |
| Adagio | | | | | | |
| sostenuto | ♩ = | 54 | 60 | 60 | 52 | 63 |
| Allegretto | ♩. = | 76 | 80 | 76 | 56 | 63 |
| Presto agitato | ♩ = | 80 | 92 | 92 | 88 | 88 |
| **Op. 28** | | | | | | |
| Allegro | ♩. = | 72 | 72 | 69 | 69 | 66 |
| *Andante | ♪ = | 84 | 88 | 104 | 84 | 84 |
| Allegro vivace | ♩. = | 96 | 100 | 100 | 96 | 104 |
| Allegro ma | | | | | | |
| non troppo | ♩. = | 88 | 88 | 92 | 84 | 80 |
| **Op. 31/1** | | | | | | |
| Allegro vivace | ♩ = | 144[34] | 152 | 160 | 138 | 160 |
| Adagio | | | | | | |
| grazioso | ♪ = | 116 | 126 | 132 | 112 | 112 |

| | Czerny 1842 | 1850 | Moscheles | Bülow | Schnabel |
|---|---|---|---|---|---|
| **Op. 31/1** (cont.) | | | | | |
| Allegretto ♩ = | 96 | 100 | 84 | 80 | 100 |
| ***Op. 31/2** | | | | | |
| Largo ♩ = | | 50 | 50 | 44 | 60 |
| Allegro ♩ = | 104 | 108 | 126 | 108 | 120 |
| Adagio ♪ = | 84 | 92 | 92 | 100[35] | 88[36] |
| Allegretto ♩. = | 76 | 88 | 88 | 80 | 69 |
| **Op. 31/3** | | | | | |
| Allegro ♩ = | 144 | 152 | 160 | 116 | 116 |
| Allegretto vivace ♩ = | 80 | 88 | 92 | 100 | 100 |
| Moderato e grazioso ♩ = | 88 | 96 | 112 | 88 | 96 |
| Presto con fuoco ♩. = | 100 | 96 | 96 | 84[37] | 100 |
| **Op. 53** | | | | | |
| Allegro con brio ♩ = | 88 | 88 | 88 | 84[38] | 88[39] |
| Adagio molto ♪ = | 56 | 60 | 60 | 60 | 44 |
| Allegretto moderato ♩ = | 88 | 100 | 112 | 108 | 112 |
| Prestissimo 𝅝 = | 88 | 84 | 80 | 76[40] | 88 |
| **Op. 54** | | | | | |
| Tempo di Menuetto ♩ = | 108 | 108 | 120 | 104 | 104 |
| Allegretto ♩ = | 144 | 120 | 108 | 138-144 | 126 |
| **Op. 57** | | | | | |
| Allegro assai ♩. = | 108 | 120 | 126 | 126 | 120 |
| Andante con moto ♪ = | 108 | 112 | 92 | 100-108 | 96 |
| Allegro ma non troppo ♩ = | 132 | 144 | 152 | 132-138 | 152 |
| Presto ♩ = | | 96 | 100 | 92-96 | 104 |

|  | Czerny 1842 | 1850 | Moscheles | Bülow | Schnabel |
|---|---|---|---|---|---|
| **Op. 78** | | | | | |
| Adagio cantabile ♪ = 72 | | 76 | 76 | 72 | 63 |
| Allegro ma non troppo ♩ = 116 | | 138 | 138 | 126[41] | 126[42] |
| Allegro assai ♩ = 132 | | 132 | 132 | 138 | 152 |
| **Op. 81a** | | | | | |
| Adagio ♪ = 63 | | 72 | 72 | 60 | 50 |
| Allegro ♩ = 112 | | 126 | 108 | 120 | 108 |
| Andante espressivo ♪ = 72 | | 72 | 72 | 72 | 63-69 |
| Vivacissimamente ♩. = 108 | | 108 | 108 | 108-112 | 120 |
| **Op. 90** | | | | | |
| Mit Lebhaftigkeit ♩ = 160 | | 198[43] | 198[44] | 152-160 | 144-152 |
| Nicht zu geschwind ♩ = 88 | | 96 | 96 | 84 | 84 |
| ***Op. 101** | | | | | |
| Allegretto ma non troppo ♩. = 72 | | 72 | 72 | 69-72 | 63 |
| Vivace alla Marcia ♩ = 152[45] | | 132 | 132 | 160[46] | 152 |
| Adagio non troppo ♪ = 60 | | 60 | 60 | 58 | 46 |
| Allegro ♩ = 132 | | 132 | 132 | 120 | 126 |
| **Op. 106** | | | | | |
| Allegro ♩ = 138 | | | 116 | 112 | 138 |
| Assai vivace ♩. = 80 | | | | 80 | 80 |
| Presto ♩ = 152 | | | | 144 | 152 |
| Adagio sostenuto ♪ = 92 | | | | 92 | 92 |
| Largo ♪ = 76 | | | | 76 | 76 |

| | Czerny 1842 | Czerny 1850 | Moscheles | Bülow | Schnabel |
|---|---|---|---|---|---|
| **Op. 106** (cont.) | | | | | |
| Allegro risoluto ♩ = | 144 | | | 138 | 144 |
| **Op. 109** | | | | | |
| Vivace ma non troppo ♩ = | 100 | 112 | 112 | 116 | 116 |
| Adagio espressivo ♪ = | 66 | 66 | 72 | 63 | 60 |
| Prestissimo ♩. = | 80 | 80[47] | 80[48] | 84-88 | 88-92 |
| Andante molto cantabile (Theme) ♩ = | 63 | 66 | 66 | 60 | 58 |
| Variation 1 ♩ = | | | | 58 | 54 |
| Variation 2 ♩ = | | 84 | 84 | 60 | 63 |
| Variation 3 ♩ = | 132 | 138 | 138 | 138[49] | 152[50] |
| Variation 4 ♩. = | | 56 | 56 | 50 | 48 |
| Variation 5 ♩ = | | 76 | 76 | 92 | 92 |
| **Op. 110** | | | | | |
| Moderato cantabile molto espressivo ♩ = | 76 | 63 | 63 | 69 | 63 |
| Allegro molto ♩ = | 120 | 112 | 112 | 126 | 144 |
| Adagio ♪ = | 66 | 69 | 69 | 63 | 66 |
| Arioso ♪ = | | 60 | 60 | 63-69 | 46 |
| Allegro ma non troppo ♩. = | 100 | 92 | 92 | 69 | 84 |
| **Op. 111** | | | | | |
| Maestoso ♩ = | 54[51] | 56 | 52 | 52 | 52-54 |
| Allegro con brio ed appassionato ♩ = | 132 | 126 | 126 | 132[52] | 138[53] |
| Adagio molto semplice e cantabile ♪ = | 63 | 60 | 60 | 48 | 48-50 |

(In comparing the metronome markings given above, a difference of two notches or more on the metronome scale will be described as "significant," in order to compensate for the possibility of a discrepancy between the metronomes used.)

Two-thirds of Czerny's metronome markings of 1850 are faster than those of the *Piano School,* eight years earlier. Of the remainder, slightly more than one-sixth of the markings of 1850 are the same as the earlier set, and slightly less than one-sixth are slower. Twelve movements are marked significantly faster, while only three are significantly slower. The movements which Czerny marked faster, for the greater part, were of a fast or moderate tempo originally. There are evidences of a tendency toward fast tempi, but these are not all that striking; curiously enough, the second movement of Op. 54, with its perpetual motion character, is marked significantly slower.

A comparison of Moscheles' markings for the Hallberger edition of 1858 with Czerny's Simrock edition reveals that a little less than one-fourth of the markings are faster, almost three-fifths are the same, and about one-sixth are slower. Applying the standard of significant difference, however, greatly increases the area of agreement, leaving only eight movements significantly faster and six slower. Compared with Czerny's earlier markings of the *Piano School,* the tendency toward faster tempi in slow movements in Moscheles becomes more apparent: nineteen slow or moderate movements (or portions of movements) have significantly faster markings than the Czerny *Piano School.* The exceptions are notable. Moscheles' tempo for Op. 10/3, II, is the same as the earlier Czerny marking ( $\flat$ = 72); since this movement was a favorite of Beethoven, both Moscheles and Czerny presumably heard him play it. Moscheles' tempo for the Funeral March of Op. 26 is considerably slower than Czerny's marking. This is also the case with the slow movement of Op. 57, for which Czerny's unusually fast tempi, $\flat$ = 108 and $\flat$ = 112, are difficult to explain. A comparison of Moscheles' markings for *scherzo* movements with those of Czerny (1842) reveals that seven are faster and five the same or slower. Of the former, the *scherzo* of Op. 27/1 and that of 31/3 are significantly faster, while of the latter, the middle movement of Op. 14/2 and the second movement of Op. 110 are significantly slower. Moscheles must have been on familiar ground in the case of Op. 110, for his wife writes in her biography:

Moscheles studied them [Op. 109 and Op. 110] with the greatest zeal, was quite absorbed in their beauties, and played them before his art brethren, and in particular to his friend August Leo, whom he credits with a genuine understanding of music, and a graceful turn for composition. Around Leo was collected a circle of Germans whose musical centre was Moscheles, and who were unanimous in their reverential homage of Beethoven.[54]

The overall trend shown in the two Czerny versions and the Moscheles version is one of increasingly faster tempi. It would be logical to assume that the earlier markings of Czerny represent tempi closer to those which Czerny played in Beethoven's presence. Individual movements for which Czerny revised the metronome markings upward include the finale of Op. 31/2, which increases from $\quad = 76$ to $\quad = 88$, and the *Grave* of Op. 13, which advances from $\quad = 92$ to $\quad = 63$. It is possible that Czerny's dislike for an unsteady tempo accounts for the much more flowing tempo at the opening of the *Pathétique*. Czerny's concept of the Rondo of the "Waldstein" and all movements of the "Appassionata" also changed considerably. It may be that Beethoven actually wanted the slow movement of Op. 57 played that fast, or that Czerny exaggerated the original direction of *con moto*. Among the less expected Moscheles markings are the slow tempi for the finales of both Op. 26 and Op. 54, each of which has a built-in fluency inviting for a virtuoso. Also noteworthy is the slower tempo of the *Andante* of Op. 57, much nearer the usual concept of the movement today. By contrast, the *Andante* of Op. 28, as it is marked by Moscheles, is disturbingly fast, the result being almost Mendelssohnian.

Marx also mentions the tendency toward faster tempos:

To be sure, the meanings of the old tempo indications have been altered; people now take the tempo much livelier. Mozart's words about the "botching" of his works through an exaggerated tempo — "They think, here it's supposed to get fiery; well, if there's no fire in the piece, it can't be put in by pushing the tempo" — this word of wisdom has not been able to hold its own against the haste of vanity and inner emptiness which feels so easy.[55]

From a discussion between Schindler and Beethoven recorded

in a conversation book after one of the rehearsals for the concert of May 7, 1824, it is clear that Beethoven's ideas about tempo had changed. Only Schindler's part of the conversation needed to be written out; Beethoven's comments were spoken.

> I would have liked to have embraced you in the rehearsal yesterday when you gave all of us the reasons why you conceive your works differently than 15-20 years ago.
>
> . . . . . . . . . . . . . . . . . . . . . . . . . . . . . . . . . . . . . . . . . . . . . . .
>
> I honestly admit that in earlier years I was often not in agreement with this or that tempo, because I felt it otherwise, that is to say, the meaning of the music.
>
> . . . . . . . . . . . . . . . . . . . . . . . . . . . . . . . . . . . . . . . . . . . . . . .
>
> It was also clearly recognizable already, and obvious to many, in the rehearsals in the Josephstadt, that you wanted *all the Allegros slower* than you had earlier. I noted the reason . . .
>
> . . . . . . . . . . . . . . . . . . . . . . . . . . . . . . . . . . . . . . . . . . . . . . .
>
> . . . a huge difference! All that which came out in the middle voices was earlier completely lost and often muddy.[56]

Schindler, whom Marx described as a man "of superior intellectual refinement," was an untiring critic of pianists who indulged in what he believed to be excessively fast tempos. One suspects that the bitterness of his attacks upon Clara Schumann, Moscheles, Mendelssohn and Liszt was generated by their success before the public. No matter what Schindler thought of their playing, he himself could not demonstrate how Beethoven should be played but instead had to content himself with publishing articles, teaching, and interviews. The complaints were not altogether unwarranted, judging by the comments of contemporary reviewers whom Schindler quotes in his biography.

The apparent tendency toward faster tempi in the Czerny-Moscheles metronome markings given above does not seem to have continued in Bülow, whose metronome markings agree more nearly with the slower Czerny markings of 1842. A comparison of tempi for slow movements, as given by Czerny (1842) and Bülow, reveals that Bülow has indicated a slower tempo for almost one out of every two slow movements, three of which are significantly slower. In the twentieth century, two-thirds of Schnabel's markings for slow movements are still slower than Bülow's, in eight instances by a rather wide margin. Furthermore, a comparison of Schnabel's metronome indications in the table above with those of Czerny (1850) and Moscheles shows a much larger proportion of faster movements than is shown by a comparison of Bülow's markings with those of Czerny-Moscheles. Therefore, the conclusion may be drawn that the preference in tempos in the quarter century after Beethoven's death leaned toward slower fast movements and faster slow movements than is customary today. This is the same conclusion at which Temperley arrived in his study of Sir George Smart's timings.[57]

It is impossible to speak with any certainty about the degree of tempo modification which Beethoven's taste demanded in playing his works. Schindler consistently emphasized the freedom in Beethoven's playing,[58] a style which Mendelssohn, after hearing the Baroness Ertmann play, described as unsteadiness. Each generation has its own standard for coherence and unity in performance which indicates to the thoughtful musician the limits he will observe in liberties taken with tempo. Beethoven's attitude is given in Marx:

> On the autograph of the song "Nord oder Süd" one can clearly read, in Beethoven's hand: "100 according to Maelzel, but this is only valid for the first measures, since feeling also has its beat, which however cannot be expressed completely by this tempo (namely, 100)."[59]

Beethoven's scores in themselves provide excellent examples of tempo modifications and free performance. If certain devices and markings are regarded as manifestations of this inner freedom, the danger of exaggeration in following the instructions left by Beethoven's students is avoided. Some of these free-tempo devices are obvious, others more subtle. Among the more obvious are the rhetorical pauses which Beethoven indicated with a fermata (Exx. 28, 29, 30). In addition to these, the finale of Op. 10/3 furnishes

Ex. 28. Op. 2/1, I, 7-9

Ex. 29. Op. 2/3, IV, 295-306

Ex. 30. Op. 7, IV, 11-12

an extended example of free tempo through rhetorical pauses. Another device illustrating free tempo is the recitative (Ex. 31).

Ex. 31. Op. 110, III, 4-7

Obviously, free performance would include a *ritardando* or a *stringendo* written in the score (Exx. 32, 33). Every cadenza is an

Ex. 32. Op. 57, I, 235-239

Ex. 33. Op. 101, III, 25-28

example of free performance, whether fast and brilliant or lingering and withdrawn (Exx. 34, 35). A certain amount of freedom is

Ex. 34. Op. 2/3, I, 232

Ex. 35. Op. 54, I, 135-138

necessary also to produce a *subito piano* after a *crescendo* (Ex. 36).

Ex. 36. Op. 28, I, 71-77

Written out embellishments in the sense of the term as it is used by Czerny in the *Piano School,* that is, to describe any kind of figuration ornamenting the melody, require just enough freedom from a metronomically even beat to avoid crowding (Exs. 37, 38). Finally, the

Ex. 37. Op. 27/1, III, 23-25

Ex. 38. Op. 81a, II, 17

freedom which Schindler described in Beethoven's playing may have been little different from the performer's interpretive response to changes in the pace of activity in the score. For example, Schindler advises a somewhat faster tempo in the A-flat minor section of the slow movement of Op. 13 where the triplet figure is first introduced in the accompaniment.[60] Czerny's suggestion of an *accelerando* in the middle section of the *Adagio* of Op. 27/2 occurs at the point where the long notes of the melody are discontinued and the triplet figure comes into the foreground (Ex. 39). Czerny's instructions read as follows:

> In measures 32 through 35 a significant *crescendo* and also *accelerando* to *forte,* which decreases again in measures 36 through 39.[61]

Ex. 39. Op. 27/2, I, 32-39

In the first movement of Op. 28, the gradual progress throughout the development section toward tension and away from it again is written in by shortening the phrases and, at the end of the section, by lengthening the note values. In the finale of the same sonata, the effect of an *accelerando* is created by note values (Ex. 40).

Ex. 40. Op. 28, IV, 181-188

Czerny emphasized the concept of freedom when speaking of Op. 53 (Ex. 41).

> As peaceful as the opening must be, at the entrance of the *fortissimo* and the triplet passage which follows the liveliness must be increased somewhat, returning to the earlier peacefulness with the return of the theme.[62]

Ex. 41. Op. 53, III, 51-62

Czerny writes of the opening *Adagio* of Op. 81a, "The last three measures ritardando."[63] In the last measure of this *Adagio,* Beethoven has suggested a change in the pace of the tempo by delaying the downbeat (Ex. 42). Czerny refers to the second variation of the

Ex. 42. Op. 81a, I, 14-16

last movement of Op. 109 as *etwas belebt.*[64] Although Beethoven has not indicated a new tempo marking for his variation, the sixteenth notes provide a marked increase of activity over the preceding variation. In another passage, from Op. 110, the change of pace from sixteenths to half-notes tied over the downbeat into eighths gives the phrase the effect of slowing down (Ex. 43).

Ex. 43. Op. 110, I, 99-105

Schindler and Czerny represent two differing viewpoints on free performance. Schindler pointed to the Baroness Ertmann's playing as a model because of her instinctive sense for giving each phrase its proper pace without distorting the whole work. For Schindler, Czerny's playing, by comparison, was too metronomically regular.

Schindler's directions for tempo modifications in Op. 13 and in Op. 10/1 may be found in his biography, *Beethoven as I Knew Him*. If these directions are followed, the result has the effect of being more personal and at the same time more dramatic, as though poetic meter were disregarded and a poem read as impassioned prose. In the *Grave* of Op. 13, Schindler, who presumably was following Beethoven's directions, asked that the contrasts between outburst and waiting, between statement and silence, be forced upon the listener's attention. Imagine the suspense of waiting on the opening *fp* chord until it has almost died away, then continuing with the dotted figure played somewhat out of rhythm, followed by a lengthened dotted sixteenth rest before the next *fp* chord. The run of quick notes at the end of measure 4 which leads into the E-flat major melody, rather than being squeezed into the last quarter beat of the measure, is interpreted by Schindler somewhat like a cadenza, while the repeated sixteenth-note chords which follow are to be played in strict, even rhythm. The high point of the *Grave* — the ascent in the right hand in measures 7 and 8 to the *fp* F-natural octave in measure 9 — was very probably the top of the compass of Beethoven's piano of that time. (This was the area of the piano's range which Hummel advised be used with caution, in order that the audience not "hear more wood than musical sound.") Beethoven's *sforzando* on this high note indicates something less than caution — and here Schindler rhetorically waits again. The *fermata* which Schindler places over the A-flat (two notes before the last) in measure 4 points out a pitch relationship with the A-flat under Beethoven's own *fermata* in measure 10.

In the *Adagio* of the same sonata, and presumably reflecting Beethoven's teaching, Schindler advises holding back the tempo in the F-minor section, beginning in measure 17, and moving ahead in the A-flat minor section, beginning in measure 37. [65]

In the earlier C-minor Sonata, Op. 10/1, Schindler states that the tempo is to be held back in the second theme of the finale until the arrival of the *fortissimo* in measure 22. Because of the different tonality of the parallel passage in the recapitulation, he goes on to say, any modification of the tempo there should be considerably less.[66]

Schindler recommends a suggestion made by Marx for holding back the tempo for emphasis at a particularly dramatic point in the first movement of Op. 31/2 (Ex. 44).[67]

Ex. 44. Op. 31/2, I, 54-69

The two chords which follow [measure 2 in the example] demand the full force of one's sound and in addition a very significant holding back, with an especially emphatic wait on the second chord (D-F-B♭), after which the quarters A G♯ A let up considerably and follow the tempo more closely.

These two chords are the peak of the excitement and power of the whole work; they must be seized and sounded out with a lion-like spirit. Thereupon the phrase is repeated an octave higher — and again a second octave higher with further melodic continuation to the cadence on *A*. This climax-motive becomes softer with each repetition and gradually returns to the first tempo — or rather almost back to the first tempo. The six measures beginning with the cadence on *A* are held back again, especially with each beginning of the motive in the bass.

With the beginning of the motive in eighths the original tempo is completely reestablished . . . .[68]

Schindler describes the tempo of this movement generally as "hesitant" and "restless," saying that the *Allegro* is not fully established until measure 15.[69]

Statements of a moderating nature made by Schindler indicate that he did not advocate unrestrained license. Using a passage from Hummel he supports his own statement that free performance was usually nothing more than a relaxation of the tempo of a cantabile section in a fast movement:[70]

> The Allegro requires brilliancy, power, precision in the delivery, and sparkling elasticity in the fingers. Singing passages which occur in it, as we have already said, may be played with some little relaxation as to time, in order to give them the necessary effect; but we must not deviate too strikingly from the predominating movement, because, by so doing, the unity of the whole will suffer, and the piece degenerate into a mere rhapsody.[71]

The excerpt from Hummel's A-minor Concerto carries explanatory remarks such as "with energy," "in an expressive and melodious style," "from here, something quicker and more marked," and "somewhat slower and in a singing style" above the brilliant or cantabile passage to which each applies. At the end of the excerpt, Hummel adds:

> All relaxation of the time in single bars, and in short passages of melody, in pleasing and intermediate ideas, must take place almost imperceptibly, and not be carried to excess, so that the difference between the remission in the time, and the natural progress of the movement may never appear too striking with regard to the original measure. The graces must be so calculated by the player, that they may neither add to nor take from the strict time, but terminate always simultaneously with the bar.[72]

Schindler refers also to subtle fluctuations of which only sensitive musicians would be aware, such as the changes of tempo in the brooding slow movement of Op. 10/3, in which Beethoven himself said the pace must be changed no less than ten times.[73] One's best guidelines are good taste and experience, Schindler adds — not emotion.[74]

The close association which Schindler had with Beethoven began almost twenty years after the period during which Czerny and

Ries studied with Beethoven. The older Beethoven may have wanted greater freedom in performance, although, according to Ries, this manner of playing was already evident at the time when he studied with Beethoven.

> In general he played his compositions very whimsically; nevertheless, he usually kept a steady beat and only occasionally pushed the tempo, and even then, seldom. Among other things he held back the tempo in his *crescendo* with a *ritardando,* which made a very beautiful and highly striking effect.[75]

If Schindler's phrase, "playing free tempo correctly," were to be reversed to read "playing correct tempo freely," it might correspond more closely to Czerny's viewpoint. Czerny, as a practical and responsible teacher, knew that modifications of tempo can easily become distortion and caricature. Consequently he warns repeatedly against dragging tempi:

> . . . the middle section of Op. 2/1, IV, "tender, with moving expression, but not dragging"[76]

. . . . . . . . . . . . . . . . . . . . . . . . . . . . . . . . . . . . . . . . . . . .

> . . . the theme of Op. 26, I, "cannot be dragged through expressive *ritardandos*"[77]

. . . . . . . . . . . . . . . . . . . . . . . . . . . . . . . . . . . . . . . . . . . .

> . . . the variation of the theme in the second half of Op. 28, II, "very legato and expressive, but not dragging"[78]

. . . . . . . . . . . . . . . . . . . . . . . . . . . . . . . . . . . . . . . . . . . .

> . . . the slow movement of Op. 31/1, because of its length, "must not be drawn out" . . . the recitative passages in the finale "not drawn out"[79]

. . . . . . . . . . . . . . . . . . . . . . . . . . . . . . . . . . . . . . . . . . . .

> . . . the second theme of Op. 53, I, "peaceful but not dragging"[80]

. . . . . . . . . . . . . . . . . . . . . . . . . . . . . . . . . . . . . . . . . . . .

> . . . the tempo of Op. 90, II, "must not drag"[81]

. . . . . . . . . . . . . . . . . . . . . . . . . . . . . . . . . . . . . . . . . . . .

> . . . the first movement of Op. 101 "neither in a dragging tempo, nor distorted through unsteady tempo"[82]

Czerny directs "strict tempo" in the slow movements of Op. 2/3 and Op. 7, because of the large number of rests, as well as in a passage from the first movement of Op. 57, (meas. 47-50), which is "already interesting through its strangeness and permits only a completely even performance in strict tempo" (Ex. 45).[83] Czerny

Ex. 45. Op. 57, I, 47-50

applied a "strict tempo" direction also to the slow movement of Op. 22, saying, "The tempo solid and definite, since the expression must be shown more through touch."[84] It is applied again to the long slow movement of Op. 106, where the "fluent and varied passages" will enliven the piece without any further modification on the part of the performer.[85]

If Czerny and Schindler differed in their approach, it would seem that in the result each desired there was no substantial difference between them. In Czerny's commentary one reads:

Here we must insert the special and generally applicable remark, that there is a positive manner of playing melodic passages more peacefully and yet not noticeably slower, so that everything seems to flow in one and the same tempo, and that a person would notice the difference at most only if he were using a metronome. One must not permit oneself an obvious change of tempo, except in such a place where the composer has expressly indicated it with a *piú lento, ritardando,* etc. [86]

Schindler even recommends that portion of Czerny's *Piano School* having to do with "free performance," entitled "On Occasional Changes in the Time or Degree of Movement." It is noteworthy that Czerny does not use the term "free performance" and that, furthermore, he begins his discussion by insisting upon strict tempo:

That Time is infinitely divisible, as well as power of tone, we have already remarked. Before everything else, we must consider it as a rule, always to play each piece of music, from beginning to end, without the least deviation or uncertainty, in the time prescribed by the Author, and first fixed upon by the Player. But without injury to this maxim, there occurs almost in every line some notes or passages, where a small and often almost imperceptible relaxation or acceleration of the movement is necessary, to embellish the expression and increase the interest.[87]

After giving an example of the various ways in which the tempo of a given phrase may be modified, Czerny lists specific situations which call for such changes. This portion of the *Piano School* (Volume III, Chapter III) is given below, along with examples from the Sonatas, to which the particular rule may be applied.

The *Ritardando,* according to the generally established rule, is much more frequently employed then the *Accelerando,* because the former is less likely to disfigure the character of the piece, than the too frequent hurrying on in the speed of movement. We may retard the time most advantageously:

a. In those passages which contain the return to the principal subject.[88]

Two applicable, but differing examples occur in Op. 2/2, I, and Op. 2/3, I; the first occurs at the beginning of the recapitulation, while the second introduces a statement of the theme within the development section (Exx. 46, 47).

Ex. 46. Op. 2/2, I, 220-227

Ex. 47. Op. 2/3, I, 107-110

In the second movement of Op. 7, the measure introducing the

B-flat major statement of the theme and the measure introducing the actual recapitulation in C major have an indication of *tenuto,* or as Beethoven often writes it, *tenute* (Ex. 48). An example of *tenuto* written in note values occurs in the third movement of Op. 27/2 (Ex. 49).

Ex. 48. Op. 7, II, 41-51

Ex. 49. Op. 27/2, III, 99-102

Czerny writes specifically of measures 78-82 of the second movement of Op. 57:

> The third variation . . . always increasing in strength and also gradually a little faster, until it descends into the theme.[89]

Ex. 50. Op. 57, II, 78-82

b. In those passages, which lead to some separate member of a melody.[90]

A *crescendo* to a *subito piano* necessitates a slight adjustment in the tempo in the first movements of Op. 28 and Op. 78 (Exx. 51, 52). Examples of this dynamic device, with a resulting disruption

Ex. 51. Op. 28, I, 87-93

Ex. 52. Op. 78, I, 10-12

of the rhythmic pulse, are very common in Beethoven's works. In Op. 28, the *subito piano* and its resultant tempo modification mark the turning point in the direction of the melody, which descends after its long insistence on D-natural. In Op. 78 the same device marks the beginning of the second variation of the *Allegro* theme. In measure 6 of the first movement of Op. 81a the articulation slurs hold back the flow of the tempo in the second half of that measure to lead into the repeat of the opening motive (Ex. 53). Considering

Ex. 53. Op. 81a, I, 6-8

Beethoven's usage of *rallentando* and *ritardando* in certain situations, it would seem that Czerny's original meaning could be expanded to include "passages which lead to a new melody" (Exs. 54, 55). In

Ex. 54. Op. 2/2, I, 48-56

Ex. 55. Op. 90, I, 50-56

a similar fashion, measure 59 which leads into the B-major theme in the second movement of Op. 90 requires a relaxation of the tempo (Ex. 56).

Ex. 56. Op. 90, II, 55-61

c. In those long and sustained notes which are to be struck with particular emphasis, and after which quicker notes are to follow.[91]

In several instances a slight lengthening of the chords is preferable to shortening them (Exs. 57, 58, 59, 60).

Ex. 57. Op. 2/2, I, 84-92

Ex. 58. Op. 7, IV, 60-64

Ex. 59. Op. 57, III, 308-310

Ex. 60. Op. 78, I, 31-34

Beethoven's use of *sforzando* over "syncopated" chords at the end of the second movement of Op. 110 seems to require a slight lengthening of the chords in preparation for the *poco ritardando* four measures from the end (Ex. 61).

Ex. 61. Op. 110, II, 143-158

d. At the transition into another species of time, or into another movement, different in speed from that which preceded it.[92]

Czerny was very sensitive about sudden changes of tempo, as the following indicates:

And as the *cres*: and *dimin*: must be executed by degrees, and with a well calculated increase or decrease in power; so also it is with the *acceler.* and *rallent.* A sudden change in slowness or quickness in single notes would in this case spoil the whole effect.[93]

This is possibly the kind of nuance of tempo which Beethoven had in mind in the development of the first movement of Op. 106 just before the entrance of the cantabile theme in B major (Ex. 62).

Ex. 62. Op. 106, I, 198-202

Holding back the tempo in measure 20 of Op. 31/2, I, would emphasize the entrance of the triplets, a point which seems to mark the real beginning of the movement (Ex. 63).

Ex. 63. Op. 31/2, I, 19-22

e. Immediately after a pause.[94]

The one example in the sonatas of Beethoven with an indication of *rallentando* after a long rest occurs in measure 302 of the fourth movement of Op. 2, No. 3 (Ex. 64).

Ex. 64. Op. 2/3, IV, 301-305

Czerny might have approved of a relaxation of tempo between measures 118 and 129 in the first movement of Op. 10, No. 2, coming as it does, as a recapitulation not in the tonic key and following a *fermata* (Ex. 65).

Ex. 65. Op. 10/2, I, 116-120

f. At the Diminuendo of a preceding very lively passage; as also in brilliant passages, when there suddenly occurs a trait of melody to be played piano and with much delicacy.[95]

A slightly slower pacing of the last three C-major chords, ending with a *fermata,* would allow time to insure that the *piano* and

Ex. 66. Op. 2/2, I, 154-162

*pianissimo* are heard in Op. 2/2, first movement (Ex. 66). Czerny suggested a more tranquil motion beginning in measure 105 in the first movement of Op. 22 (Ex. 67).[96] According to Czerny's directions, it might also be appropriate to relax the tempo in measure 44 of Op. 10/3, IV (Ex. 68). The *forte* should presumably continue

Ex. 67. Op. 22, I, 104-108

Ex. 68. Op. 10/3, IV, 41-45

until the beginning of measure 112 of Op. 90, second movement, allowing one measure for a *diminuendo* to a *pianissimo*. This could be accomplished more easily if the tempo were held back somewhat in measures 112 and 113 (Ex. 69).

Ex. 69. Op. 90, II, 110-115

g. In embellishments, consisting of very many quick notes, which we are unable to force into the degree of movement first chosen.[97] [See Exx. 70, 71, 72, 73.]

Ex. 70. Op. 10/1, II, 75-78

Ex. 71. Op. 13, I, 4, 10

(At the end of the second measure of Example 71 Schindler added a *ritenuto* and a *fermata*.)

Ex. 72. Op. 31/3, I, 53-57

Ex. 73. Op. 111, I, 118-119

Considering Czerny's tempi for the first movement of Op. 31/3 ( ♩ = 144 and ♩ = 152), it is difficult to see how his indication could be followed: "The run which follows very light and fast, but in tempo."[98]

> h. Occasionally also, in the chief *crescendo* of a strongly marked sentence, leading to an important passage or to the close.[99]

Ries' statement that Beethoven at times "held back the tempo in his *crescendo* with *ritardando*" corroborates Czerny's suggestion. An excellent example occurs in the first movement of Op. 78; in measure 24 Beethoven wrote *tenute* over the chords in the left hand to aid in holding back the tempo during the *crescendo* (Ex. 74).

Ex. 74. Op. 78, I, 24-27

At the peak of the excitement in the development section of Op. 57, Beethoven wrote a "braking" device into the figure, shortening the broken chord in the left hand and increasing the length of wait at the end of the figure (Ex. 75).

Ex. 75. Op. 57, I, 123-126

In addition to the fact that the passage introduces the recapitulation, the combination of sustained harmony, a *crescendo, sforzandi* on the off-beats, and ending with a dotted half-note under a *fermata,* implies a broadening of the tempo in measures 179-183 of the first movement of Op. 10/3 (Ex. 76).

Ex. 76. Op. 10/3, I, 179-184

Czerny suggests that the *forte* measures (50, 52) in the third movement of Op. 27/2 be "held back significantly and played very staccato" (Ex. 77).[100]

Ex. 77. Op. 27/2, III, 49-52

However, in many instances in his commentary on the playing of the Beethoven piano works, Czerny recommends that an *accelerando* be coupled with a *forte* or a *crescendo,* or both. The *crescendo* and *diminuendo* accompanied by an *accelerando* and return to tempo in the middle section of the *Adagio* of Op. 27/2 was mentioned earlier. Of measures 23-29 and 71-76 of the slow movement of Op. 10/3 (Exx. 78a, 78b), Czerny writes:

> In this Largo a well calculated *ritardando* and *accelerando* must enhance the effect. Thus, for example, the second half of measure 23 is to be played somewhat faster, as is the second half of measure 27 and all of measure 28. Likewise an increase of liveliness and force in measures 71 to 75 before returning to the original level of peacefulness in measure 76.[101]

Ex. 78a. Op. 10/3, II, 23-29 *According to Czerny*

Ex. 78b. Op. 10/3, II, 71-76

Czerny writes of the *Adagio* of Op. 31/2 (Ex. 79):

> It must not move tediously, and the tempo must be kept steady... In measure 55 *crescendo* to *forte,* and *accelerando*, then measure 58 *piano* and *rallentando*.[102]

Ex. 79. Op. 31/2, II, 55-59 *According to Czerny*

i. In very humorous, capricious, and fantastic passages, in order to heighten the character so much the more.[103]

Both Schindler and Czerny speak of the capricious manner in which the second theme of the finale of Op. 10/1 is to be played. Czerny says that it is accomplished "through a whimsical retarding of single notes."[104] When Czerny speaks in his commentary of *jenem fantastischen Humor* of this movement, *Humor* should be translated as mood rather than as humor in the sense of jesting.

k. Lastly, almost always where the Composer has indicated an *espressivo* . . .[105]

An interesting aspect of Beethoven's use of the term *espressivo* is that he often repeats the term at exactly the same point in the parallel passage later in the movement, possibly indicating that the direction applies only to the measures or phrase over which it is written — as would be the case with a *ritenuto* (Ex. 80). Czerny

Ex. 80. Op. 2/1, I, 41-48

says of this passage that, from the second half of measure 41 through measure 44, it is to be played with "increasing ritardando," after which the tempo of the movement returns in measure 45.[106]

The *espressivo* of measure 50 in the exposition of the first movement of Op. 81a is also repeated at the same point in the parallel passage (Ex. 81).

Ex. 81. Op. 81a, I, 50-51

Like examples 80 and 81, the *espressivo* marking in the first movement of Op. 109 recurs at exactly the corresponding passage. It is possible that the indication applies only to slurred thirty-seconds under which it stands and not to the unslurred notes which follow (Ex. 82).

Ex. 82. Op. 109, I, 14, 63

In the second movement of Op. 109, *un poco espressivo* is followed by *a tempo,* a clear indication of a tempo modification (Ex. 83).

Ex. 83. Op. 109, II, 29-33

In Op. 101, Beethoven indicates *poco espressivo* simultaneously with *dolce; dolce* describes the character, while *poco espressivo* is an indication to hold back the tempo a little (Ex. 84).

Ex. 84. Op. 101, III, 239-241

In editing the Sonata, Op. 27/1, Moscheles added *espressivo* simultaneously with *un poco piu moderato* at a point in the finale, followed by *Tempo I* at the return of the theme (Ex. 85). The presence of both directions suggests that the pianist of 1858 may no longer have understood *espressivo* as a tempo marking.

Ex. 85. Op. 27/1, IV, 139-143. *According to Moscheles*

*Espressivo,* used in a movement marking, presumably indicates "free performance." This is supported by the visual appearance of the first variation in the last movement of Op. 109 — the many appoggiaturas, the detailed directions for articulation, the numerous tied notes in the melody line, and the dynamic markings within single beats (Ex. 86).

Ex. 86. Op. 109, III, Variation 1

*Espressivo* also appears in the tempo marking for the first movement of Op. 110. At one point, the term appears with *a tempo* following *ritenente,* indicating that "Tempo I" and *espressivo* are inseparable in this movement (Ex. 87).

Ex. 87. Op. 110, I, 78-80

1. At the end of every long shake which forms a pause or Cadenza, and which is marked diminuendo.[107]

Whether Czerny's suggestion should be applied to measures 160-161 in the last movement of Op. 111 is open to question. Extending the trill would afford the player more time to achieve a real *diminuendo* and prepare the final *pianissimo* (Ex. 88).

Ex. 88. Op. 111, II, 159-161

Further on in the same section dealing with modifications of tempo, Czerny adds: "Sudden transitions into another key, must also be marked by a change in time."[108] This would probably apply to the abrupt intrusion of C major in measure 53 of the second movement of Op. 2/3. Whether slower or faster would depend upon the taste of the player (Ex. 89).

Ex. 89. Op. 2/3, II, 52-55

 Time is experienced both as a quantity measured by the beat of a metronome and as a quality, a kind of time-forgetting, based upon that which occupies our attention. Music is psychological time, an intensified experience of the quality of time, in which the sense of the passage of time is lost.

 Tempo is neither marking time nor distorting it. A runner is aware of the rhythm of his body movements and his heartbeat which enables him to run the race, although the pace of this rhythm varies as it is influenced by subjective experiences during the race, such as the firmness of the track, the presence of spectators, the performance of other runners, and fatigue. Tempo modification is the result of the musician's subjective experience of musical events within measured time, in the course of which, like the runner, he loses sense of time and enjoys the exhilaration of the race.

# Notes and Sources

## Chapter II

[1]Anton Schindler, *Beethoven as I Knew Him,* edited by Donald W. MacArdle (Chapel Hill: The University of North Carolina Press, 1966), p. 423.

[2]Carl Czerny, *Vollständige theoretisch-practische Pianoforte-Schule, Op. 500* (Vienna, 1842), Vol. IV, p. 72.

[3]*Ibid.,* p. 120.

[4]Emily Anderson, *The Letters of Beethoven* (New York: St. Martin's Press, 1961; London: Macmillan & Co.), Vol. II, p. 727.

[5]Schindler, p. 161.

[6]Czerny, *Pianoforte-Schule,* Vol. IV, p. 62.

[7]*Ibid.,* p. 121.

[8]Nicholas Temperley, *Tempo and Repeats in the Early Nineteenth Century* (in *Music and Letters,* October, 1966), Vol. 47, No. 4, pp. 323-336.

[9]*Encyclopaedia Britannica* (New York, 1911), Vol. 18.

[10]Czerny, *Pianoforte-Schule,* Vol. IV, p. 66.

[11]Schindler, p. 425.

[12]Gustav Nottebohm, *Beethoveniana* (Leipzig and Winterthur, 1872), p. 127.

[13]Czerny, *Pianoforte-Schule,* Vol. IV, p. 35.

[14]*Encyclopaedia Britannica,* Vol. 18.

[15]Schindler, pp. 425-426.

[16]Anderson, Vol. III, p. 1325.

[17]Albert Dreetz, *Czerny und Beethoven* (Leipzig: Kistner & Siegel, 1932), p. 17.

[18]Nottebohm, p. 136.

[19]Alan Tyson, *Moscheles and his 'Complete Edition' of Beethoven* (in *Music Review,* May, 1964), Vol. 25, No. 2, p. 140.

[20]Given as $\quarternote$ = 50 in Moscheles.

[21]Given as $\quarternote$ = 144 in Bülow.

[22]Given as ♩ = 152 in Schnabel.

[23]Given as ♩ = 50 in Moscheles.

[24]Given as ♪ = 132 in Czerny (1850).

[25]Given as ♪ = 138 in Moscheles.

[26]Given as ♩ = 160 in Czerny (1850).

[27]Given as ♩ = 160 in Moscheles.

[28]Given as ♪ = 92 in Czerny (1842).

[29]Given as ♩ = 160 in Moscheles.

[30]Given as ♩ = 160 in Czerny (1850).

[31]Given as ♩ = 160 in Moscheles.

[32]Given as ♩ = 138 in Bülow.

[33]Given as ♩ = 160-168 in Schnabel.

[34]Given as 𝅗𝅥 = 72 in Czerny (1842).

[35]Given as ♩ = 50 in Bülow.

[36]Given as ♩ = 44 in Schnabel.

[37]Given as ♩. = 168 in Bülow.

[38]Given as ♩ = 168 in Bülow.

[39]Given as ♩ = 176 in Schnabel.

[40]Given as ♩ = 152 in Bülow.

[41]Given as 𝅗𝅥 = 63 in Bülow.

[42]Given as 𝅗𝅥 = 63 in Schnabel.

[43]Given as 𝅗𝅥. = 66 in Czerny (1850).

[44]Given as 𝅗𝅥. = 66 in Moscheles.

[45]Given as 𝅗𝅥 = 76 in Czerny (1842).

[46]Given as 𝅗𝅥 = 80 in Bülow.

[47]Given as ♩. = 160 in Czerny (1850).

[48]Given as ♩. = 160 in Moscheles.

[49]Given as 𝅝 = 69 in Bülow.

[50]Given as 𝅝 = 76 in Schnabel.

[51]Given as ♪ = 108 in Czerny (1842).

[52]Given as 𝅝 = 66 in Bülow.

[53]Given as 𝅝 = 69 in Schnabel.

[54]Charlotte Moscheles, *Life of Moscheles* (London, 1873), pp. 60-61.

[55]Adolf Bernhard Marx, *Anleitung zum Vortrag Beethovenscher Klavierwerke* (Berlin, 1875), p. 62.

[56]Marx, p. 63.

[57]Temperley, p. 335.

[58]Schindler, p. 412.

[59]Marx, p. 69.

[60]Schindler, p. 499.

[61]Czerny, *Pianoforte-Schule,* Vol. IV, p. 51.

[62]*Ibid.,* p. 59.

[63]*Ibid.,* p. 63.

[64]*Ibid.,* p. 68.

[65]Schindler, pp. 497-499.

[66]*Ibid.,* p. 401.

[67]*Ibid.,* p. 401.

[68]Marx, p. 126.

[69]Schindler, p. 402.

[70]*Ibid.,* p. 412.

[71]Johann Nepomuk Hummel, *A Complete Theoretical and Practical Course of Instruction in the Art of Playing the Piano Forte* (London, 1827), p. 41.

[72]*Ibid.,* p. 47.

[73]*Schindler,* p. 421.

[74]*Ibid.,* p. 499.

[75]F. G. Wegeler and F. Ries, *Biographische Notizen über Ludwig van Beethoven* (Coblenz, 1838), p. 106.

[76]Czerny, *Pianoforte-Schule,* Vol. IV, p. 36.

[77]*Ibid.,* p. 49.

[78]*Ibid.,* p. 53.

[79]*Ibid.,* p. 54.

[80]*Ibid.,* p. 58.

[81]*Ibid.,* p. 64.

[82]*Ibid.,* p. 65.

[83]*Ibid.,* p. 61.,

[84]*Ibid:,* p. 48.

[85]*Ibid.,* p. 66.

[86]*Ibid.,* p. 95.

[87]Carl Czerny, *Complete Theoretical and Practical Piano Forte School* (London, 1839), Vol. III, p. 31.

[88]*Ibid.,* p. 33.

[89]Czerny, *Pianoforte-Schule,* Vol. IV, p. 61.

[90]Czerny, *Piano Forte School,* Vol. III, p. 33.

[91]*Ibid.,* p. 33.

[92]*Ibid.,* p. 33.

[93]*Ibid.,* p. 33.

[94]*Ibid.,* p. 33.

[95]*Ibid.,* p. 33.

[96]Czerny, *Pianoforte-Schule,* Vol. IV, p. 47.

[97]Czerny, *Piano Forte School,* Vol. III, p. 33.

[98]Czerny, *Pianoforte-Schule,* Vol. IV, p. 57.

[99]Czerny, *Piano Forte School,* Vol. III, p. 33.

[100]Czerny, *Pianoforte-Schule,* Vol. IV, p. 51.

[101]*Ibid.,* p. 44.

[102]*Ibid.,* pp. 55-56.

[103]Czerny, *Piano Forte School,* Vol. III, p. 33.

[104]Czerny, *Pianoforte-Schule,* Vol. IV, p. 42.

[105]Czerny, *Piano Forte School,* Vol. III, p. 34.

[106]Czerny, *Pianoforte-Schule,* Vol. IV, p. 35.

[107]Czerny, *Piano Forte School,* Vol. III, p. 34.

[108]*Ibid.,* p. 37.

# III

# *Dynamics*

SOUND IS the raw material of music, and differences in degrees of loudness and softness constitute the most primitive contrast possible in music. Whether it is speech, sounds of nature, warning signals, noise, or the organized patterns called music, the sensuous qualities of sound are the immediate determinants of response. That Beethoven's ideas were "incited by moods, which are translated . . . into tones that sound, and roar and storm about me until I have set them down in notes" indicates that he was never far from his raw material.[1] Czerny's statement that "With him every sound, every movement became music and rhythm" explains how the "fusion of imaginative experience and reality" — a characteristic of the Storm and Stress — was effected on a musical plane.[2]

Beethoven's revolutionary treatment of dynamics is due to his employment of raw sound as a structural element. By way of definition, Beethoven's sound may be considered "raw" in those passages where the harmonic movement is static and only dynamic contrast holds the listener's attention (Exx. 90, 91, 92). Beethoven's use of raw sound must have been far more striking during improvisation than in the finished composition. According to Schindler, when Beethoven improvised for himself he often extended his left hand and produced such a jumble of sound in the bass that whatever he may have been playing with the right hand was hardly distinguishable.[3]

Ex. 90. Op. 31/3, I, 127-138

Ex. 91. Op. 57, I, 15-24

Ex. 92. Op. 110, III, 131-136

Beyond the fact that the foregoing passages exemplify "raw" sound "set down in notes," examples 90, 91, and 92 illustrate three instances in which dynamics implement structural aspects of a work. In the first movement of Op. 31/3 (Ex. 90), it was one matter to begin the movement "in the air" — in a sense, to start without a beginning — but it is a far more difficult matter to make the recapitulation occur in such a way that it gives the same impression. To accomplish this, Beethoven led to an F-minor chord as inconspicuously as possible by means of chromatic alterations. He then prolonged that chord, using a *crescendo,* until the static quality of the chord as a color important in itself had been established (Ex. 90). The first sixteen measures of the first movement of Op. 57 comprise quasi-introductory material ending with a half cadence on the dominant of F minor. To continue in the same key with basically the same material, and, at the same time, create the impression of a new "beginning," Beethoven's solution was based on dynamic contrast — a violent interruption of F minor *pianissimo* with F minor *fortissimo,* as though with great effort the piece were now moving on to something different (Ex. 91). In the passage from Op. 110 (Ex. 92), the transition from the second *Arioso* to the continuation of the fugue in inversion occurs at a point where the piece is moving from darkness to light, from G minor to G major, and from a thick texture to a lighter one. Since both the end of the *Arioso* and the beginning of the fugue are played *una corda,* Beethoven appears to have believed that some dramatic touch was needed — in this case, the G-major chords repeated with a *crescendo* over a long pedal — to establish a new beginning point from which the fugue may continue.

In each of these examples, patches of what may be called "nonmusic" or "raw sound" produce a psychological response which enables the listener to accept these passages as points of reorientation. This use of dynamic contrast becomes a kind of signpost saying, "Watch, something important is going to happen." A dynamic indication in the opening measures of the third movement of Op. 27/2 constitutes the "key" to discovering the relationship between the outer movements of the sonata (Ex. 93). The chords under the

Ex. 93. Op. 27/2, III, 1-4

*sforzando* may be regarded as a musical exclamation point which reveals a series of features in which the first and last movements of the sonata are alike:

> 1) The point in the bar, the fourth beat, on which the *sforzando* chords in the opening measures of the finale and the upbeat figure in the melody in the first movement are placed.
>
> 2) The predominance of the pitch G-sharp in both cases.
>
> 3) The prominence of broken-chord figuration in both movements.
>
> 4) The similarity in the descent of the bass from tonic to dominant at the beginning of both movements.
>
> 5) The presence of similar motivic material in both movements (Ex. 93a).

Ex. 93a

> 6) In each movement, the use of the same tonality, F-sharp minor, at the opening of the development section, followed by an extended G-sharp pedal point closing the same section.
>
> 7) The placement of the theme of the first movement and the second subject of the finale (this time also suspended from a G-sharp) in the left hand at the beginning of the coda of both movements.

It seems reasonable to conclude that the outer movements of this sonata constitute two variations of a large, never-stated *Ur-pattern*.

In the third volume of the Piano School, Czerny speaks of the "determinate character of dynamic levels" in a manner that reveals his preoccupation with psychological reaction:

a. The Pianissimo (pp) which indicates the gentlest touching of the keys, so however, as not to become indistinct or inaudible. It bears the character of secrecy, mystery, and when executed with the utmost perfection, it is capable of producing on the hearer the pleasing effect of music at a great distance, or of an echo.

b. The Piano (p) Loveliness, Softness, tranquil equanimity, or quiet sorrow, manifest themselves by the still, soft and tender, the yet somewhat firm and expressive mode of touch with which the keys are to be struck.

c. The Mezza voce (m. v.) This degree lies exactly in the middle between soft and loud, and may be compared to the tranquil speaking tone used in narration; and without descending into a whisper or declaiming in a loud tone, it will interest us more by the matter to be played, then by the style of the performance.

d. The Forte (f) denotes the expression of self-sufficing firmness and power, without excess or presumption; Passion within the limits of proper dignity; as also, according to rule, whatever is brilliant and showy, may be executed with this degree of power.

e. The Fortissimo (ff) That even the highest degree of force must always rest within the limits of what is *beautiful,* and never be allowed to degenerate in a coarse thumping, or ill treatment of the instrument, has already been said. Within these bounds, it expresses the exaltation of joy to extacy, of grief to rage; just as it also elevates what is brilliant to absolute splendor and *Bravura.*[4]

There is no reason to doubt that Czerny's words were not far removed from the thinking of Beethoven, whose psychological states pushed every expressive means to the limit of its possibilities. In speaking of Beethoven's style in another chapter of the same volume, Czerny mentions its "characteristic and impassioned energy, alternating with all the charms of smooth and connected cantabile," adding that the "means of Expression is often carried to excess . . ."[5]

Carrying expressiveness to excess has been generally cultivated out of contemporary playing. This is due in large part to the development of the piano, which has long provided the dynamic power which Beethoven's piano did not have. Forcing the present-day instrument to produce sound beyond that which is readily available not only seems unnecessary, but a misuse of the tone quality of a really fine piano. While it would be incorrect to say that Beethoven was disinterested in beautiful piano sound, the "carrying to excess" to which Czerny referred must have had a near shattering effect on the earlier instrument and, therefore, offered another expressive means in moments of extreme agitation. Because of this, Beethoven's intent must have seemed much larger than his instrument's capacity to express it. This would have been due not only to the proportion of exertion from the player to the sound produced, but also would have been related to the size of the room in which the performance took place. While it can be argued that the shift from a less sonorous, less brilliant piano in a small room to a more sonorous, more brilliant piano in a large hall should not disturb dynamic proportions, the distance from the player to the farthest listener has a direct bearing upon audience attention. An audience somehow is more involved listening to a speaker in a small room, perhaps because he is within range of the listener's voice, while far less personal contact is sensed with a speaker on a rostrum in a large hall. Beethoven's sonatas disappeared from the repertoire shortly after his death principally because sonatas were regarded as suitable for house concerts but not for concerts in large recital halls. In large halls, where a recital partakes somewhat of a spectacle, both the sense of intimacy and the extremes of dynamic levels are easily lost. As a result, Schindler might have said of much modern playing, as he did of Kalkbrenner's, that the tone was unvaryingly loud.[6]

It is worth noticing also, with respect to the limitations of the Beethoven piano and the greater sonority of the piano which followed, that the Moscheles edition shows many instances of extending Beethoven's original *crescendo* by beginning it earlier (Exx. 94-97). Beethoven was obviously more economical with his effects; a shorter *crescendo* on his piano was more convincing than a longer one. (In these and all subsequent examples marked "according to Moscheles" or "according to Czerny," the original Beethoven dynamic indication which has been omitted or altered by the respective editor has been marked with a slash.)

Ex. 94. Op. 26, II, Trio. *According to Moscheles*

Ex. 95. Op. 27/1, IV, 266-278. *According to Moscheles*

Ex. 96. Op. 53, I, 106-112. *According to Moscheles*

Ex. 97. Op. 57, I, 146-151. *According to Moscheles*

In Volume IV of the *Piano School,* in a section dealing with conditions for achieving a spiritual concept of Beethoven's works, Czerny indicates that, especially in the later works, Beethoven marked his scores very carefully. The Beethoven letters also contain numerous and bitter complaints about the carelessness of copyists and performers in observing dynamic markings. After satisfying the requirements of strict observance of all such indications, Czerny continues, there are a host of expressive possibilites "which the player ought to infuse into his performance from the impulse of his own feelings."[7] While Czerny's detailed directions for dynamic shading and voicing of chords are proof of his experience and thoroughness as a teacher, these qualities were not always present in Beethoven's playing. An anecdote, dating from the late Bonn years, relates Beethoven's meeting with Abbé Sterkel, a particularly refined pianist whose playing Ries described as rather effeminate. According to Wegeler, the Abbé was the first great pianist whom Beethoven had heard, and the genteel style of his performance revealed a new musical dimension to Beethoven. The young Beethoven, entranced by Sterkel's playing, stood attentively beside him as he played and immediately afterward played for the gathering in the same refined manner he had just heard.[8]

In the remainder of this discussion of dynamics all the examples differ to some degree from the appearance of the particular passage in an *Urtext* edition, although each of the sources for the markings given either knew Beethoven, or studied with him, or heard him play. The examples fall into two large groups, those which presume to carry out Beethoven's intentions where indications are missing in the score and those which alter or deviate from his original markings. The question of whether a particular example should be placed in one group or the other — whether it deviates from the intention of Beethoven's original marking or not — must often be decided arbitrarily.

The examples in the first group of markings, those which presume to convey Beethoven's intentions, are distributed under five headings:

1) The assumption that Beethoven intended the same dynamic marking at each appearance of the theme.

Ex. 98. Op. 14/1, III, 121-131. *According to Moscheles*

From its position near the end of the movement and the lower dynamic marking at which it alone begins (*pp*), this last, varied appearance of the theme in Op. 14/1, third movement, seems more convincing on the withdrawn level of Beethoven's original marking, without a *crescendo*. After the immediately preceding *fortissimo,* the prolongation of the *pianissimo* through four and one-half measures has the effect of suspending activity in preparation for the *crescendo-forte* at the end (Ex. 98).

Ex. 99. Op. 31/3, II, 62-70. *According to Moscheles*

Mocheles has transferred the *sforzandi* from the beginning of the movement to each appearance of the theme in the development section of Op. 31/3, second movement. Yet Beethoven may have intended to associate the original *sforzando* with the theme only in a particular tonality — A-flat major (Ex. 99).

2) The assumption that Beethoven intended a change of dynamic level between two like dynamic markings or in a passage having only one marking.

According to his contemporaries, Beethoven's performance of unmarked measures did not remain as uninflected as the printed page would indicate. Czerny writes of Op. 2/1, IV (Ex. 100): "From measure 35 to measure 39 *crescendo* and the right hand very *cantabile*."[9]

Ex. 100. Op. 2/1, IV, 34-40. *According to Czerny*

Considering the fact that Czerny actually studied Op. 14/1 with Beethoven, the *crescendo-diminuendo* indication in the second to fourth measures of the first movement ( ⟨⟩ ) may well have been an additional direction which he received from Beethoven (Ex. 101).[10]

Ex. 101. Op. 14/1, I, 1-4. *According to Czerny*

Beethoven's original markings for Variation 2 of the first movement of Op. 26 include two *piani,* a *crescendo*, two *rinforzandi* and a *sforzando*. Moscheles' extensive editing of the variation suggests that he was a sensitive pianist who cultivated the control of dynamic shading in his playing (Ex. 102). The *crescendo* indication ($<$) and *p* in measure 94-95 are taken from Beethoven's original markings for the theme. Of the dynamics in this variation, Czerny says only: "In the last eight measures the *crescendo* goes to a *forte;* however, the last four measures are once more to be played lightly *staccato* and very softly."[11]

Ex. 102. Op. 26, I, Variation 2. *According to Moscheles*

Beethoven indicated no dynamic change between the *piano* in measure 100 and the *crescendo* in measure 124 of Op. 26, IV, yet Moscheles, in his intent to make the "finest nuances clear to the amateur," added *cresc.* in measure 103 and *p* in measure 106 (Ex. 103), as well as frequent dynamic swells. Czerny says of this movement: "It must have interest through evenness of touch and shading of the rising and falling movement, without stepping out of character

Ex. 103. Op. 26, IV, 99-128. *According to Moscheles*

with an over-sensitive interpretation or a brilliant bravura performance.''[12]

Beethoven may very well have provided the dynamic indications
for one of the most interesting passages pertaining to this discussion
(Op. 27/2, I, 32-41). Moscheles suggests the same dynamic swell
throughout the measures over this dominant pedal, without, however, indicating a *forte* climax. Czerny writes that the *una corda,*
which Beethoven otherwise held down throughout the movement, is
to be raised at the *forte* (Ex. 104).[13]

Ex. 104. Op. 27/2, I, 32-41. *According to Czerny*

Moscheles borrowed a *crescendo-piano* in measures 73-75 of Op. 31/2, I, from the parallel passage in the recapitulation (the marking found in both the Henle and Vienna *Urtext* editions). Czerny's concept of the section is quite different: "The bass passage (from measure 69) *legato,* at first *piano,* but a big *crescendo* up to *forte* (measure 75), which lets up first in measures 83-86" (Ex. 105).[14]

Ex. 105. Op. 31/2, I, 62-87. *According to Czerny*

The lack of dynamic change throughout a long passage in Op. 31/2, III (meas. 107-150) is difficult to explain since Beethoven gave detailed indications in the remainder of the movement. Although the uninterrupted *forte* seems appropriate to maintain unremitting driving energy, Moscheles' *piano* in measure 126 does provide an opportunity to heighten the effect of the long ascent to *fortissimo* twenty measures later (Ex. 106).

Ex. 106. Op. 31/2, III, 107-150. *According to Moscheles*

Individual taste will provide the determination whether to accept Moscheles' markings in some passages (Ex. 107). The interpretation might also be made that, in some instances, Beethoven does not always try to communicate with the listener and, at such times, prefers a stillness not to be disturbed by the addition of expressive swells.

Ex. 107. Op. 81a, I, 6-14. *According to Moscheles*

3) The assumption that Beethoven intended a *crescendo* or *decrescendo* before an indicated *forte* or *piano,* respectively.

Instances occur of the unmistakable omission of a *crescendo*; for example, the increase of activity in the right hand just before the *forte* in measures 118-120 of Op. 14/2, I, makes a continued *piano* illogical (Ex. 108).

Ex. 108. Op. 14/2, I, 115-124. *According to Moscheles*

Moscheles' suggestion of an early *crescendo* in measure 204 of Op. 31/3, I, disturbs the suspended quality of the broken tonic chord and the surprise of a sudden *crescendo-forte* (Ex. 109).

Ex. 109. Op. 31/3, I, 202-208. *According to Moscheles*

One can only speculate whether Beethoven intended the *forte* in measure 174 of Op. 53, I, to be sudden or prepared by a *crescendo* (Ex. 110).

Ex. 110. Op. 53, I, 171-174. *According to Moscheles*

In Op. 78, I, measure 63, the *crescendo* which Moscheles has added makes the entrance of the E-major section sound as though it were the goal of the modulations of the preceding measures. Without the *crescendo,* the sudden *forte* makes the same section seem like a new beginning in a new direction (Ex. 111).

Ex. 111. Op. 78, I, 60-66. *According to Moscheles*

In several instances, Moscheles preferred a smoother dynamic transition to Beethoven's apparent *subito* indications (Exx. 112, 112a).

Ex. 112. Op. 78, II, 22-26. *According to Moscheles*

Ex. 112a. Op. 78, II, 85-90. *According to Moscheles*

4) The setting of dynamic levels for new sections where

the composer has omitted a marking of his own (Exx. 113, 114).

Ex. 113. Op. 2/1, II, 16-17. *According to Moscheles*

Ex. 114. Op. 10/2, III, 1-4. *According to Moscheles*

In two of three other such examples found in the Moscheles edition, the marking was also *mezzo forte.*

5) The application of a rule of common practice requiring a *crescendo* in ascending passages, a *decrescendo* in descending.

This rule, as it is given in the Czerny *Piano School,* states: "According to the general rule, every ascending passage must be played *crescendo,* and every descending passage, *diminuendo.*"[15] The same statement is made by Hummel in his *Piano School,*[16] as well as by Marx in his *Anleitung zum Vortrag Beethovenscher Klavierwerke,* which Schindler recommended so highly:

> . . . in most cases phrases which rise will require a heightening of intensity, and those which fall a letting up. For rising in pitch [and] increase in intensity and speed are related, almost synonymous expressions of an intense state of mind, — and so falling in pitch [and] letting down in intensity and speed, the expression of a calming state of mind.[17]

After this, Marx discusses the application of this maxim to the theme of Op. 13 with typical German thoroughness, giving detailed directions for a *crescendo* which drops down and begins again in the second octave-segment of the theme. Both Czerny and Moscheles add a *crescendo* to the theme (Ex. 115). Since both Czerny and

Ex. 115. Op. 13, I, 11-19. *According to Moscheles*

Moscheles played this sonata in their youth, and since Czerny definitely studied it with Beethoven, it seems reasonable to assume that, if Beethoven had not desired a *crescendo,* Czerny would have said so. If this *crescendo* is acceptable, the one which Czerny added in the first two measures of the finale of Op. 27/2 should also be acceptable.[18]

The dynamic marking in the early measures of Op. 101, III, which also follows the practice of using a *crescendo* in a passage in which the uppermost voice ascends, may have been based on Moscheles' recollection of the Baroness Ertmann's playing of this sonata.

Ex. 116. Op. 101, III, 5-7. *According to Moscheles*

Both Moscheles and Czerny add a *crescendo* to the ascending theme of the first movement of Op. 10/3. In actuality it would be difficult not to play a *crescendo* here, due to Beethoven's doubling in octaves (Ex. 117).

Ex. 117. Op. 10/3, I, 1-4. *According to Moscheles and Czerny*

Of the beginning of the Trio of Op. 2/3, III, Czerny says: "The left hand heavy and the half notes always *crescendo* as they rise and *diminuendo* as they descend" (Ex. 118).[19]

Ex. 118. Op. 2/3, III, Trio. *According to Czerny*

The examples in the second group of markings, those which alter or deviate from Beethoven's original markings, are distributed under four headings:

1) Changes which differ from Beethoven's original markings but in all probability are based on verbal instructions from Beethoven himself.

Schindler, for example, states that the publisher of the original edition of the *Sonata Pathétique* omitted many dynamic marks which Beethoven intended.[20] One of these, which may have originated in Beethoven's own instructions given during a lesson, prescribes a *forte* for each of the four-note figures which the right hand crosses over to play in the bass (Ex. 119).[21] It is reasonably certain

Ex. 119. Op. 13, I, 51-53. *According to Schindler*

that Schindler studied this sonata with Beethoven, since one of the conversation books from the year 1820 contains an entry to that effect.[22]

2) Alterations having to do with the avoidance of a *subito piano* (Exx. 120-127, each according to Moscheles).

Ex. 120. Op. 14/1, III, 2-4

Ex. 121. Op. 27/1, I, 49-51

Ex. 122. Op. 28, I, 361-367

Ex. 123. Op. 28, II, 85-88

Ex. 124. Op. 31/1, I, 104-109

Ex. 125. Op. 31/2, III, 317-320

Ex. 126. Op. 53, I, 41-42

Ex. 127. Op. 109, III, 7-8

3) Alterations having to do with the avoidance of that which is unattainable on the piano or technically labored.

Ex. 128. Op. 7, II, 39-40

Ex. 129. Op. 7, IV, 62-63

Ex. 130. Op. 81a, I, 251-253

Moscheles omitted markings such as those requiring a *crescendo* during a sustained note (Ex. 128-130). Of passages such as these Philipp Emanuel Bach wrote, "There are many things in music which, not fully heard, must be imagined."[23]

Moscheles' dynamic markings for the long expanse of uninterrupted *forte* in the finale of Op. 31/2 (Ex. 106) may have been based on a personal opinion that such a lengthy section of repetitive two-part writing sounded labored rather than loud. On the other hand, he may have heard the passage played thus by one of Beethoven's pupils. It would also be defensible to reject both possibilities and regard this as another instance of Beethoven forcing his piano to display its maximum intensity.

4) · Alterations for which there is no distinct reason.

Moscheles' dynamic marking for the opening of Op. 31/1, I, matches the level of the recapitulation (Exx. 131a, b, c, d).

Ex. 131a. Op. 31/1, I, 1-16. *According to Moscheles*

Ex. 131b. Op. 31/1, I, 44-54

Ex. 131c. Op. 31/1, I, 111-116

Ex. 131d. Op. 31/1, I, 191-201

In his *Textkritische Untersuchungen bei Beethoven,* Paul Mies enters into a detailed discussion of the proper dynamic level for the opening of this sonata. Noting that the opening scale passage returns *forte* in measures 11-14, again at the first ending of the exposition, and *fortissimo* at the recapitulation — besides the fact that all appearances of the motive in the development are played *forte* — he advances the opinion that both the opening statement (meas. 1-3) and the same passage in measures 45-48 should be played *forte* as well. Mies speculates that in the manuscript the *forte* at the beginning was missing and that the engraver simply moved the *piano* in measure 3 to the beginning. Consequently, since no *piano* is actually indicated there, one might mistakenly continue the *forte* of the first ending through the syncopated motive in measure 3 (  ). Mies also questions the *forte* in measure 48, since the *forte* which appears four measures later makes the earlier one seem superfluous. This earlier *forte,* he believes, should be replaced with a *piano.*[24]

In the *Biographische Notizen,* Ries described the proofreading of the Sonatas, Op. 31/1 and 2:

> ...As the proof sheets arrived, I found Beethoven writing. "Play the sonata through," he said to me, during which he remained seated at his writing desk. There were an unusual number of mistakes in it, causing Beethoven to become very impatient. At the end of the first Allegro of the Sonata in G major, however, Nägeli had inserted four measures, specifically after the fourth measure following the last fermata:

As I played this, Beethoven jumped up angrily, came running over and half pushed me from the piano, shouting: "Where the devil is that?" — One can hardly imagine his amazement and his anger as he saw it printed thus. He gave instructions to make a list of all the errors and on the spot to send the sonatas to Simrock in Bonn, who was to copy the engraving and to add: *Edition très correcte.*[25]

Moscheles, in his edition of this sonata, included the same four spurious measures to which Ries referred, as well as the changes in dynamic level given above in Ex. 131. These may have constituted the unusual number of other mistakes Beethoven found in Nägeli's proof of the movement. It is therefore just as reasonable to argue that the dynamics for the theme (the *piano* in measures 1-3 and again in measures 45-48) as given in the Urtext editions used today (Kalmus, Henle, Vienna Urtext) represent the corrected version which Ries was instructed to send to Simrock. In such a case, the *forte* in measure 48 has the appearance of having been inserted during the proofreading to replace the *piano* which Beethoven and Ries had found in that measure.

In support of these markings, it may be pointed out that the *piano* marking is found where the left hand plays a *staccato* chord on the downbeat, while in the *forte* and *fortissimo* entrances, the corresponding downbeat is either an octave or a note low in the bass held for a full quarter, or, in measures 11-14, a dotted quarter at the beginning of a unison passage.

The reason for the substitution of *piano* for *forte* in measure 48 of Op. 109, I, may have been a concern for the quality of the piano's tone in a high register (Ex. 132).

Ex. 132. Op. 109, I, 47-49. *According to Moscheles*

There seems to be no one distinct reason for some alterations (Exx. 133-134).

Ex. 133. Op. 10/1, III, 1-5. *According to Moscheles*

Ex. 134. Op. 53, I, 68-73. *According to Moscheles*

The performer who feels persuaded that Beethoven was explicit in his indications of dynamics cannot seriously consider any of the Moscheles editings except those omissions, either editorial or Beethovenian, which Moscheles supplied. On the other hand, if the interpreter places importance on the report that Beethoven played his own works whimsically and differently each time, Moscheles' dynamic markings offer many alternatives.

Because Moscheles was a fluent pianist he may have preferred to avoid Beethoven's frequent indications of *crescendo* to *subito piano*. Since the indication is so common in Beethoven's scores, it would seem strange if he had not intended it to be played. If Beethoven's style of improvising was characterized by sudden changes of direction in the ordering of his musical ideas, it is logical that sudden and unexpected interruptions of dynamic continuity would also have been part of his style.

# Notes and Sources

## Chapter III

[1]Friedrich Kerst, *Beethoven: The Man and the Artist, as Revealed in his own Words,* edited and translated by Henry Edward Krehbiel (New York: Dover Publications, 1964), p. 29. Reprinted through permission of the publisher.

[2]Carl Czerny, *Vollständige theoretisch-practische Pianoforte-Schule, Op. 500* (Vienna, 1842), Vol. IV, p. 56.

[3]Anton Schindler, *Beethoven as I Knew Him,* edited by Donald W. MacArdle (Chapel Hill: The University of North Carolina Press, 1966), p. 385.

[4]Carl Czerny, *Complete Theoretical and Practical Piano Forte School* (London, 1839), Vol. III, p. 5.

[5]*Ibid.,* p. 100.

[6]Anton Schindler, *Für Studirende von Beethoven's Clavier-Musik* (in *Niederrheinische Musik-Zeitung,* 1853-1867), No. 45, p. 158.

[7]Czerny, *Piano Forte School,* Vol. III, p. 1.

[8]*Thayer's Life of Beethoven,* revised and edited by Elliot Forbes (Princeton: Princeton University Press, 1967; Princeton Paperback, 1970), Vol. I, p. 103.

[9]Czerny, *Pianoforte-Schule,* Vol. IV, p. 36.

[10]*Ibid.,* p. 46.

[11]*Ibid.,* p. 49.

[12]*Ibid.,* p. 50.

[13]*Ibid.,* p. 51.

[14]*Ibid.,* p. 55.

[15]Czerny, *Piano Forte School,* Vol. III, p. 15.

[16]Johann Nepomuk Hummel, *A Complete Theoretical and Practical Course of Instruction in the Art of Playing the Piano Forte* (London, 1827), p. 42.

[17]Adolf Bernhard Marx, *Anleitung zum Vortrag Beethovenscher Klavierwerke* (Berlin: Janke, 1875), p. 55.

[18]Czerny, *Pianoforte-Schule,* Vol. IV, p. 51.

[19]*Ibid.,* p. 39.

[20]Schindler, *Beethoven as I Knew Him,* p. 69.

[21]*Ibid.,* p. 500.

[22]*Ibid.,* p. 446.

[23]Carl Philipp Emanuel Bach, *Essay on the True Art of Playing Keyboard Instruments,* translated and edited by William J. Mitchell (New York: W. W. Norton & Company, 1949), p. 106.

[24]Paul Mies, *Textkritische Untersuchungen bei Beethoven* (Bonn: Beethoven House, 1957), pp. 117-119.

[25]F. G. Wegeler and F. Ries, *Biographische Notizen über Ludwig van Beethoven* (Coblenz, 1838), pp. 88-89.

# IV

# *Declamatory Style, Accentuation, Slurs and Touches*

SCHINDLER SAID of Beethoven's playing that is was

> ... the clearest and most intelligible declamation, as one could perhaps only learn, to such a degree, from a study of his works. — Particularly what the Sonata Pathétique became under Beethoven's hands had to be heard and heard again in order to convince oneself that it was the same, familiar piece.[1]

Beethoven was anything but a miniaturist, Schindler explained, playing his works instead in the manner of an orator.[2] According to Schindler, certain features of this style — the rhetorical pause, the *caesura,* an accentuation based on poetic meters, and a particular concept of touch — were adopted from Clementi. In his article, *Für Studirende von Beethoven's Clavier-Musik,* in the *Niederrheinische Musik-Zeitung,* he spoke of Clementi's contribution to the art of piano playing:

> As a self-taught singer, he attempted to carry over the prosody of the language and the rules of verbal and sung declamation into instrumental forms. Through this he arrived at the point where his playing itself became singing, and in certain works, where the representation of a particular state of the soul was called for, as for example his *Didone abban-*

*donata,* was shaped into understandable speech. Clementi showed me the indispensable necessity, for an expressive performance, of knowing with each melody which of the various verse meters, of which music makes use, could be put to the melody, whether the iambic, trochaic, etc., because of the shifting of the main accent and the caesura, of which one must take note also in the performance of instrumental music, above all in *free* performance.[3]

The idea of declamatory performance was not new. Philipp Emanuel Bach mentioned it in the *Essay* as being better suited to the style of the keyboardist than to the style of any other performer.[4] Beethoven increased the extent to which this preoccupation with the speaking quality of playing was carried, reflecting a desire for a kind of Rousseauian naturalness, for realism, and for individuality. The two devices of the declamatory style to which Schindler devotes his attention almost exclusively are the rhetorical pause and the *caesura.* While his explanation of the two terms is not very precise, with the help of Marx the *caesura* may be defined as a break or pause produced by the shortening of the last note of a phrase, while the rhetorical pause is the lengthening of a note or rest.

Schindler's discussion of the rhetorical pause and *caesura* in the first movements of Op. 10/1 and Op. 13, given in his *Beethoven as I Knew Him* (to which the reader is referred),[5] deals principally with the lengthening of rests to set apart a section of differing character (Ex. 135), or to heighten the abrupt, "torn-off" gesture

Ex. 135. Op. 10/1, I, 116-121

of separate short phrases (Ex. 136). Schindler also advises a rhetori-

Ex. 136. Op. 10/1, I, 13-22

cal pause on the dominant harmony in the thirteenth measure before the end of the exposition, again to set apart the less agitated character of the twelve-measure coda. In the *Allegro* of the first movement of Op. 13, Schindler interprets the bar line at both the beginning and the end of the E-flat minor section as a *caesura* for the purpose of emphasizing the newness of the passage. Neither these *caesurae,* nor what Schindler calls a rhetorical pause before the F-minor section of the *Adagio,* nor the *caesura* before the A-flat minor section pose any particular problems — however misleading the terminology tends to be — if the intent of the device is kept in mind: to define more clearly the opposition in character between individual sections and themes.

Schindler lists a number of early sonatas in which similar examples of Beethoven's rhetorical phrasing may be found.[6] In many instances the rhetorical pause or the *caesura* was written in by Beethoven with a *fermata* or a rest (Ex. 137).

Ex. 137. Op. 2/1, I, 7-9

A lengthening of the rests in measures 186-189 of Op. 7, I, contributes to a *ritardando* which, according to Czerny's teaching, is appropriate in a passage providing a return to the principal subject (Ex. 138). Any letting up at this point would increase the sound-

Ex. 138. Op. 7, I, 183-189

and-energy effect of the theme, which predominates over its melodic and harmonic interest. In Op. 7, III, Beethoven set off the C-flat

major section (which begins and ends *pianissimo*) with additional rests (Ex. 139). In Op. 7, IV, the obvious intent of the pause in

Ex. 139. Op. 7, III, 51-70

measure 154 is to separate the dreamy, withdrawn character of the digression into E major from the preceding train of thought which then returns seven measures later (Ex. 140).

Ex. 140. Op. 7, IV, 152-160

At several points in his commentary, Czerny speaks of the necessity of keeping a strict tempo throughout a slow movement which has many rests. Although measures 17-23 of Op. 10/1, II, could certainly be described as declamatory or rhetorical, lengthening each of the rests separating the figure would soon destroy the coherence of the movement (Ex. 141). The rhetorical pause in

Ex. 141. Op. 10/1, II, 17-23

Ex. 142 is clearly notated by the composer.

Ex. 142, Op. 10/1, III, 14-17

Schindler's treatment of the measure before the coda in the exposition of the first movement of Op. 10/1 is similar in effect to measure 41 of Op. 10/1, III (Ex. 143). The *fortissimo* on the last quarter-note in the bar, which is then tied over, has the effect of a rhetorical pause. A *caesura* would be suitable after the *fermata* in

Ex. 143. Op. 10/1, III, 40-43

measure 57 of Op. 10/1, III, just before the beginning of the reprise.

Ex. 144. Op. 10/1, III, 54-57

There seems little doubt in measure 22 of Op. 10/3, I, that a *caesura* should separate the F-sharp octaves from the beginning of the B-minor section (Ex. 145). The rhetorical pause has already

Ex. 145. Op. 10/3, I, 21-23

been written into measure 132 from the same movement (Ex. 146).
After the *fermata,* a *caesura* before the *fortissimo-piano* chord would
enhance the surprise.

Ex. 146. Op. 10/3, I, 131-134

    In their determination to give instrumental playing the character
of singing and ultimately, during "singular states of the soul," to
give it the character of speech, Clementi, Schindler, and Beethoven
all refer to the application of meters of verse to musical accentuation.
Clementi directed that "in passages and runs the long and short
accents must have audible nuances, even if they have not been
written in."[7] For his nephew Karl's study, Beethoven chose twenty
of the Cramer *Studies,* providing written directions for practice in
which he specifically tried to apply the long and short accents used
in scanning poetry to groups of notes in figurations. As an example,
in the first study Beethoven expressly directed that the first and third
notes of each group of four sixteenths be lengthened, but not to the
extent of making these notes dotted. Later when the tempo is increased, he maintained, the rhythmic unevenness would disappear
(Ex. 147).[8] In the comments for another study. Beethoven explained

Ex. 147.

that the melodic movement within the passage becomes apparent
by an observance of the long and short accents, without which a

run has no meaning.[9] This is also the gist of a statement by Schindler in discussing Clementi's teaching:

> He brought to my attention that in performance, especially of four-voice writing, the note that carries the melody, in whatever voice it may be, must be brought out; likewise that in passages and runs the melodic skeleton, which may often lie deeply hidden in melismas and embellishments, is to be stressed with the kind of tone which is a part of and which supports bass figures — otherwise the passage would become empty tinkling.[10]

In certain passages Beethoven marked the melodic outline with *staccato* accents (Exx. 148, 149) and with *sforzandi* (Ex. 150).

Ex. 148. Op. 13, I, 93-99

Ex. 149. Op. 109, III, 169-170

Ex. 150. Op. 111, I, 67-69

Tonic and dominant triads provide the scaffolding for passages like that in measures 23-29 of the "Waldstein." Whether this outline is melodically important depends upon the relationship one sees between the triad pattern at this point and the melody which appears

Ex. 151. Op. 53, I, 23-29

near the end of the exposition (Ex. 152). No doubt Beethoven's

Ex. 152. Op. 53, I, 76-78

manner of practice as given in his comments on the Cramer *Studies* would insure that this melodic outline is heard. It may also have made the student listen to inner phrasing, the stress within the beat pulling the line forward (Ex. 153).

Ex. 153.

In the *Piano School,* Czerny gave practical rules for "musical accent or emphasis as applied to single notes." Nothing is said of poetic meters, and Czerny thus spares himself and his readers a great deal of ambiguity. Notes of "longer duration," he writes, are to receive emphasis:

Any note of longer duration than those which immediately go before or follow it, must be played with greater emphasis than those shorter notes.[11]

Ex. 154. Op. 22, II, 75-77

If, in addition to accenting the A-flat in measure 76 of Op. 22, II, there is a phrasing lift — as indicated by the slur —between F and E-flat, the passage is heard as dominant harmony which goes unresolved through three repetitions of the figure. If instead the slur is continued into the E-flat each time, the effect is that of a resolution repeated three times (Ex. 154).

> *Dissonant chords* . . . are generally struck with somewhat more emphasis . . .

> As it is one of the first duties of a Player never to leave the hearer in doubt as to the subdivision of the bar, it follows of course that where it is possible, he should mark by a gentle accent the commencement of each bar, and even of every . . . subdivision of it.[12]

Czerny's comment corroborates Beethoven's insistence on the stress of the rhythmic accent in the Cramer *Studies,* as well as Schindler's observation on the presence of a strong rhythmic accent in Beethoven's playing.[13]

> All syncopated notes must be struck with peculiar emphasis [Ex. 154a].

Ex. 154a.

The same thing is to be understood when the syncopated notes stand singly.[14]

In his commentary on the playing of the Beethoven piano works, Czerny calls attention to syncopation in the *Adagio* of Op. 10/1, saying that it should be "rather marked" (Ex. 155).[15] It seems

Ex. 155. Op. 10/1, II, 91-94

curious that Czerny assigned such a fast metronome marking to the third variation in the first movement of Op. 26, the character of which seems to demand the *tenuto* effect of the syncopation (Ex. 156). In the *Adagio molto* of the "Waldstein," Beethoven pushes the

Ex. 156. Op. 26, I, Variation III

natural emphasis on the syncopated notes still farther with *sforzandi* (Ex. 157). The syncopated chords from a passage in the first move-

Ex. 157. Op. 53, II, 9-11

ment of Op. 101 give the impression of an accumulation of weight and tension (Ex. 158). The effect of the syncopation in the melody

Ex. 158. Op. 101, I, 81-88

line resembles a written *rubato* in measures 9-11 of **Op. 110, III** (Ex. 159).

Ex. 159. Op. 110, III, 9-11

The preceding examples occur in a slow or moderate tempo. In the passage given in Ex. 160, as in the third variation of Op. 26, I (Ex. 156), the syncopated notes are held, while those on the beat are *staccato*. A *tenuto* on the syncopation holds back a fast tempo just as it encourages lingering in a slow one (Ex. 160).

Ex. 160. Op. 2/3, I, 203-206

The first of the two notes which are here connected together by a short slur, must always be struck with a somewhat marked accent . . . [Ex. 160a]

Ex. 160a.

The marks of expression which are affixed to single notes, require those notes to be played *one* degree louder than they would otherwise be.[16]

If this advice is followed the *sforzandi* at the end of Variation 5 in the last movement of Op. 109 would not be louder than *mezza voce* (Ex. 161). Nevertheless, Czerny also stated that in Beethoven

Ex. 161. Op. 109, III, 148-152

"the means of expression is often carried to excess . . . "[17]

Every note which is to be held down for some time, particularly in the treble and in pp and p passages, must be struck with some little degree of emphasis. . . .

With the same sort of emphasis must every higher note of a melody be played, as compared with those which are deeper as to pitch.[18]

Czerny writes of measure 19 of Op. 2/3, II: "The right hand accompanies with a clear legato and with a single stress on the highest note" (Ex. 162).[19] In the *Adagio* of Op. 27/2, Czerny calls

Ex. 162. Op. 2/3, II, 19-20

attention to the highest note in the melodic figure: "In the 15th [really the 16th] measure the c♮ with particular meaning" (Ex. 163).[20]

Ex. 163. Op. 27/2, I, 15-17

When a simple trait of a melody is repeated several times, we can vary the accentuation of it in many different ways, and thus cause it to appear always new and interesting.[21]

Of the second movement of Op. 90 Czerny says in his commentary: "Since the theme recurs often, the player must strive to throw it into relief by playing it each time, however delicately, with different nuances."[22]

In chords the highest notes must be more strongly marked than the rest, especially when those notes form a melody.[23]

Referring to voicing, Czerny writes of measures 103-112 of Op. 2/3, IV: "The middle section (in F major) is to be played *legatissimo* and *cantabile* and the melody lying on top to be brought out well. Thus also later the left hand" (Ex. 164).[24]

Ex. 164. Op. 2/3, IV, 103-112

Before leaving the subject of accentuation, mention should be made of Czerny's comment regarding the finale of Op. 26:

The two eighth-notes     in the left hand in measure six are to be pointed out with a single accent, and similarly wherever they occur in a cadence or a half-cadence, for example, in measures 12, 20, 28, 30, 32, 34, *etc.* One finds often in Beethoven's works that he bases the structure of his composition on single notes which appear unimportant and that when one makes these notes prominent (as Beethoven himself did) the whole receives the proper color and unity.[25]

Czerny's example seems relatively obscure. In numerous in-

stances Beethoven placed an accent over the particular note that he
wished to be given prominence. Often this note is the dominant,
and the effect is that of establishing a stationary point to which
melodic and rhythmic activity is anchored. For example, the *ffp*
in Op. 2/2, I (Ex. 165), recalls the prominence of the pitch E at

Ex. 165. Op. 2/2, I, 202-211

the beginning of the sonata (Ex. 165a) as well as the open-ended

Ex. 165a.

close on the dominant within the theme itself (Ex. 165b). In other

Ex. 165b.

Ex. 166. Op. 10/3, II, 36-40

Ex. 167. Op. 28, I, 219-226

instances, the single note so accented colors the tonality of the passage. In the A-flat theme of the exposition of the first movement of Op. 2/1, the F-flat gives the major tonality a minor cast (Ex. 168).

Ex. 168. Op. 2/1, I, 20-22

The tonality of the theme of the *Allegro* of the first movement of the *Pathétique* in ambiguous. Much of it is strongly F minor (over a C pedal), while the C-minor resolution of measure 13 is changed immediately to major (Ex. 169). One may speculate that the E♭ —

Ex. 169. Op. 13, I, 11-15

E♮ relationship in this theme was developed from the E♭-D-E♮ — F motive which appears in the *Grave* (Ex. 169a), and which is

Ex. 169a. Op. 13, I, 4

then pounded out at the limits of Beethoven's keyboard at the close of the development (Ex. 169b). The conclusion that the conflict

Ex. 169b. Op. 13, I, 181-183

between E♭-E♮ is a structural balance point for the movement gains credibility in the light of Beethoven's respelling of the E♭ as D♯ just preceding the return of the *Allegro* in E minor in the development (Ex. 169c). Perhaps as a consequence of this

Ex. 169c. Op. 13, I, 135-136

harmonic move, Beethoven adds a *sforzando* to the C-major side of the theme at the recapitulation (Ex. 169d).

Ex. 169d. Op. 13, I, 195-197

For a discussion of eighteenth-century practice in the performance of slurs, the reader is referred to the chapter on articulation in
the Badura-Skodas' *Interpreting Mozart on the Keyboard*. Beethoven's use of slurs represents a mixture of earlier and contemporary
practice. The older notation for a long legato — slurs extending
from barline to barline — is retained in the second theme of the
first movement of Op. 31/3 (Ex. 170). At other times Beethoven

Ex. 170. Op. 31/3, I, 49-53

used a long slur extending over several measures (Ex. 171). Marx,

Ex. 171. Op. 57, I, 186-189

whose *Anleitung zum Vortrag Beethovenscher Klavierwerke* Schindler recommended, illustrates the realization of articulation slurs in
Beethoven — short slurs indicating stress and lift within melodic
segments of a phrase — using passages from the first movement of
Op. 90 and the *Adagio* of Op. 106.

> . . . the two-measure organization continues in effect and
> finds its expression in the shortening of the tones marked
> with the sign (†), which, according to the purport of the
> slurs, are to be lifted off a little ( ♪ ⸲ or ♪. ⸲ ); each seg-
> ment begins with a slight emphasis and ends diminuendo,
> as it is even indicated in the last segment.[26] [Ex. 172]

Ex. 172. Op. 90, I, 8-15

At times the organization [division of phrase segments] lies more deeply hidden, as for example in the Adagio of the great B-flat major Sonata, Op. 106, where, not counting the introductory first measure, unmistakable segments of 4 and 4, then of 2 measures etc. (shown by the sign † †) stand out; however, smaller units also (marked with †) could be rendered clear by a pause or by a letting-up in the tone.[27] [Ex. 173]

Ex. 173. Op. 106, III, 1-13

The German which Marx uses to express "a pause or letting-up in the tone" is *Absatz oder Nachlass der Schallkraft*.[28] In his explanation of the performance of the examples above, Marx indicates that *Absatz* and *caesura* are synonymous.

Czerny gave explicit directions concerning the execution of the slurs in particular passages in the Beethoven piano works. He wrote as follows about the slurs in the Scherzo of Op. 28: "The two eighths torn off very short, without being connected to the following quarter" (Ex. 174).[29] The result is rhythmically distorted, as Czerny's advice

Ex. 174. Op. 28, III, 1-8

on the slurred sixteenths in Op. 78 indicates: "The separated sixteenths very quick, played almost like grace notes" (Ex. 175).[30]

Ex. 175. Op. 78, II, 12-16

To this may be added Czerny's identical directions for playing the theme of the Rondo of the C-major Concerto:

> In this theme the 2 sixteenths must be separated to such an extent that the second of the two will be torn off and in no way connected with the following eighth. Therefore more

this way:  than this:[31]

Of a similar figure in the first movement of the G-major Concerto Czerny writes:

> The following phrase:

> is to be played very softly and lightly, but at the same time the second sixteenth in the first 2 measures played short and quickly broken off, approximately like this:[32]

In the second movement of Op. 78 one would assume that, like the separated pairs of sixteenths, the two-note slurred-figures in the theme — as well as the motive in the first movement from which this theme is derived — should be played in the same sharply separated manner, even though Czerny's slurring does not indicate this (Exx. 176a, b). The slurred pairs of sixteenths in the finale of Op. 81a might possibly also be played in a manner approaching grace notes (Ex. 177). Beethoven's remark that the slurred eighths in measures

Ex. 176a. Op. 78, II, 1-8

Ex. 176b. Op. 78, I, 31-34

Ex. 177. Op. 81a, III, 9-10

2-5 of Op. 31/2, I, should sound as though one were dusting the keys indicates that style was always a more important consideration than a literal execution (Ex. 178).[33] The so-called *Bebung* device

Ex. 178. Op. 31/2, I, 1-5

Ex. 179. Op. 106, III, 165

in Beethoven is nothing more than a two-note slur on the same pitch (Ex. 179). Czerny described the performance of the opening of Op. 27/1, II: "The three quarters of each measure are to be separated *legato* in such a manner that the third quarter always appears torn away somewhat *staccato*" (Ex. 180).[34] The rule given by C.P.E. Bach in the *Essay* that notes of broken chords under a slur are to be held down, if applied to this passage, will produce the peculiar gasping effect consistent with the character of the movement (Ex. 180).[35]

Ex. 180. Op. 27/1, II, 1-8

Because the "sustained style" was an important feature of Beethoven's manner of playing, broken chords under short slurs, in many instances, should probably be held down (Exx. 181, 182, 183).

Ex. 181. Op. 27/2, III, 7-9

Ex. 182. Op. 31/1, I, 162-165

Ex. 183. Op. 13, III, 1-8

In an instance like that in the third movement of Op. 27/2, the broken chord is written to be held down (Ex. 184).

Ex. 184. Op. 27/2, III, 163-164

The notation and types of touches which Beethoven inherited may be summarized as follows:

1) A slur indicated *legato,* meaning that notes under it were to be held their full value.

2) Absence of a slur, as well as of any other direction for

articulation or touch, indicated a *non legato,* meaning that such notes were held for less than their full value.

3) A wedge or a dot over a note indicated that it should be played *staccato.* Türk states that both signs have the same meaning, although "some wish to indicate a shorter *staccato* by means of the wedge."[36] Bach seems anything but pedantic about the difference, saying that he used the dot in the *Lessons* to avoid confusion with fingering numerals. The brevity of the *staccato,* he reasoned, depended upon the length of the note, the tempo, and the dynamic level.[37]

In considering Beethoven's thinking on touches, two facts must be kept in mind: one, that he constantly sought to produce as many gradations of each effect as possible,[38] and two, that he wanted his indications to be well defined in performance. The latter is demonstrated in Czerny's commentary by the frequent use of words like "as possible" or "extremely," as well as other phrases demanding clear differentiation:

Op. 2/1, IV . . . "Beginning with measure 22 in the first part, both hands extremely *legato.*"[39]

. . . . . . . . . . . . . . . . . . . . . . . . . . . . . . . . . . . . . . . . . .

Op. 2/2, II . . . ". . . the lower voice to be played as *staccato* as possible, but softly."[40] (At each appearance of the theme Beethoven has indicated *tenuto sempre* for the right hand and *staccato sempre* for the left.)

. . . . . . . . . . . . . . . . . . . . . . . . . . . . . . . . . . . . . . . . . .

Op. 2/2, II . . . ". . . each voice must be well differentiated from the other."[41]

. . . . . . . . . . . . . . . . . . . . . . . . . . . . . . . . . . . . . . . . . .

Op. 2/2, IV . . . "The middle section (A minor) is to be played very powerfully and in both hands as *staccato* as possible up to the point where it is repeated *pianissimo* and very *legato.*"[42]

. . . . . . . . . . . . . . . . . . . . . . . . . . . . . . . . . . . . . . . . . .

Op. 26, I, Variation 4 . . . ". . . the left hand as detached as possible."[43]

Beethoven expressed himself far more frequently about *legato* than other touches. He told Czerny that Mozart had a detached, *non-legato* style of playing,[44] for which he (Beethoven) had a strong dislike, calling it a "finger dance."[45] Czerny added that Beethoven himself had developed the same touch through his early training on the organ. To improve his *legato,* Beethoven spoke of playing a slurred passage as though each note were stroked with a bow rather than struck with a hammer.[46] For Beethoven a means of disguising the percussive nature of the instrument was the "sustained style," consisting of overholding certain notes in the melody, as well as chord tones within figuration. Schindler remembered that Beethoven held down certain notes in Op. 14/2, I (F-sharp in measure 15, A-natural in measure 17) and used a "soft, gliding touch" (Ex. 185). In Op. 14/1, I, Schindler also mentions Beethoven holding the A-natural on the third beat of measures 7 and 8 of Op. 14/1, I (Ex. 186).[47]

Ex. 185. Op. 14/2, I, 14-18

Ex. 186. Op. 14/1, I, 7-10

The sustained style which Beethoven prescribed in his comments on the Cramer *Studies* is also intended to point out the progression of melodic line within figuration. Cramer's original version and that recommended by Beethoven for practice are placed side by side (Ex. 187). Beethoven's explanatory comments are reproduced in Huber's *Beethoven's Anmerkungen zu einer Auswahl von Cramer-Etuden* (Hug & Co., Zürich), which is, unfortunately, out of print.

Ex. 187.

Czerny, like his teacher, gives much attention to *legato,* stating that:

> . . . it must be employed in all cases where the Author has not indicated any particular expression. For in music, the Legato is the rule, and all other modes of execution are only the exceptions.[48]

Of *legatissimo* Czerny says that it is "applicable only to arpeggioed chords" and that one must be careful to hold down "only such notes belonging to those chords as are consonant or agreeable to the ear."[49] In the sense of overholding note values, Czerny's treatment of *legatissimo* is therefore similar to the sustained style (Ex. 188).

Ex. 188.

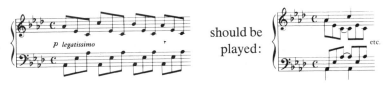

should be
played:

In similar fashion the Czerny *Piano School* illustrates that, in a *legatissimo,* consonant notes forming a chord are to be overheld (Ex. 189).

Ex. 189.

At all crotchets and minims, the fingers *after the percussion,* must keep the keys firmly down, as low as they will descend.

In the first three bars, the notes of the melody in the right hand must be held down so long, that each finger shall not quit its key, till somewhat after the next note is struck, say not till after about the length of one of the quavers of the accompanying triplets. The two last triplets in the third bar, and the three last triplets in the fifth bar are to be held as long in the right hand as each finger can possibly remain stationary on its key.[50]

In the finale of Op. 28, because of the indication *molto legato* in addition to the short slurs over the broken chords, it may be assumed that Beethoven intended all the notes of each chord to be held down (Ex. 190).

Ex. 190. Op. 28, IV, 17-19

Czerny stresses *legato* to just as great an extent in his commentary on the Beethoven piano works. The word *legato* appears more often than any other technical or interpretive indication. In addition to melodic and broken chord patterns, Czerny applies *legato* to chords (Ex. 191). Czerny writes of this passage: "The chords in

Ex. 191. Op. 13, I, 5-9

general very heavy, and in measures 5-8, the accompaniment in the

Ex. 192. Op. 22, II, 33-35

left hand very *legato*."[51] And, of measures 34 and 35 of Op. 22, II, he writes: "In the second section the duo which alternates from one voice to the other clearly marked and the accompaniment *legatissimo*."[52] Czerny uses the term *tenuto* in referring to the chords in the Funeral March of Op. 26:

> As a funeral march on the death of a hero this movement must be played with a certain serious bigness, which emerges not only from the slow stride of the tempo but also from a heavy touch on the chords in the strictest *tenuto*, by means of which the full-voiced quality of these chords is apparent in every degree of *piano* and *forte*.[53]

In spite of his dislike for the *non legato* of the preceding generation, it would be wrong to assume that Beethoven did not explore all

the gradations of touch between *legato* and *staccato*. In measures
19 and 23 of Op. 109, II, (Ex. 193), the addition of the word
*legato* in those measures where previously only a slur had been used

Ex. 193. Op. 109, II, 9-24

(meas. 11, 15) not only indicates that Beethoven wished to preserve
the integrity of each voice part and avoid a careless performance
such as Ex. 193a might represent, but also implies that the measures

Ex. 193a.

on either side were to be played *non legato*. Care must be exercised
in accepting at face value Czerny's general statement that *legato*
"must be employed in all cases where the Author has not indicated
any particular expression." Slurs are rare in the finale of Op. 57,
of which Czerny wrote, "The passages are to be played with clear
evenness and lightness, little *legato,* and only rarely stormy."[54]
Likewise the passages of sixteenths and thirty-seconds in the *Adagio*
sections of the first movement of Op. 109 — for the most part also
unslurred — are to be played "very lightly, like dream figures, just
as the *Vivace* is effective only very *legato* and singing."[55]

The apparent correlation between lightness and *non legato* is also real, for Czerny specifically mentions it in the *Piano School.* He refers to two species of *mezzo staccato,* the first of which is better known as *portato* and, according to Czerny's organization of his material, occurs in a slow tempo.

> When, however, runs and passages still quicker than these are to be played in this manner, the *second species* of mezzo staccato playing must be employed; it consists in this, that each finger with its soft and fleshy tip on the keys, makes a motion like that used in scratching or in tearing off something . . . and thereby obtains a very clear, pearly, and equal touch, by which, even in the quickest times, all passages may be executed with equal roundness and finish, with a full and not too harsh a tone, and with the most perfect and pleasing tranquility of the hands.

> All passages distinguished by the words *Leggiermente,* or *Leggierissimo,* must be executed in this manner; as well as the most tasteful embellishments, particularly those in the higher octaves, which receive thereby a particularly charming effect.[56]

In some instances, not only has Beethoven left the passage unslurred, but he has also marked each one *leggiermente* (Exs. 194, 195, 196).

Ex. 194. Op. 31/1, II, 13

Ex. 195. Op. 79, I, 12-16

Ex. 196. Op. 110, I, 18-19

*Leicht,* or *Leichtigkeit,* which appears very frequently in Czerny, is treated on occasion as the equivalent of *leggiermente* to describe an unslurred passage which seems to require *non legato* (Ex. 197).

Ex. 197. Op. 2/2, IV, 16-18

This *Rondo,* to be played moderately *Allegro,* demands a tender and sensitive expression and a graceful lightness in the passages.[57]

Of measures 51-53 of the slow movement of Op. 31/2, Czerny indicates that: "The passages in the left hand light and soft, so that the melody may stand out *legato*" (Ex. 198).[58]

Ex. 198. Op. 31/2, II, 51-53

Friedrich Starke, in his *Wiener Pianoforte-Schule* (1820), distinguishes between three types of *staccato*:

1) the short, sharp *staccato,* which is indicated by dashes, and by which each note is held for one-fourth of its value;

2) the half *staccato,* which is indicated by dots and requires that the note is held for half its value;

3) the sustained *staccato* (*appoggiato*), which is indicated by dots under or over a slur, by which each note is held for three-fourths of its value.[59]

Clementi, in his *Introduction to the Art of Playing the Pianoforte,* is less exact in prescribing the difference in length between the three *staccato* marks:

> The best general rule, is to keep down the keys of the instrument the FULL LENGTH of every note; for when the contrary is required, the notes are marked either thus: ʼ called in ITALIAN, STACCATO; denoting DISTINCT-NESS, and SHORTNESS of sound; which is produced by lifting the finger up, as soon as it has struck the key: or they are marked ʼ which when composers are exact in their writing means LESS STACCATO than the preceding mark; the finger, therefore, is kept down somewhat longer: or thus ʼ ʼ ʼ which means STILL LESS staccato: the nice degree of MORE and LESS, however, depend on the CHARAC-TER, and PASSION of the piece; the STYLE of which must be WELL OBSERVED by the performer.[60]

In the *Piano School* Czerny writes merely that the *staccatissimo* is indicated "by perpendicular dashes or strokes over the notes, which in playing must be carefully distinguished from the dots which frequently occupy the same situation."[61]

In a letter written to Karl Holz in August, 1825, regarding corrections to the A-minor Quartet, Beethoven asked that dots over notes be replaced by dashes, since the two signs did not have the same meaning.[62] Beethoven's corrections on a set of orchestral parts for the A-major Symphony indicate a like desire for precise differentiation. Where a copyist had placed dots (Ex. 198a), Beethoven

Ex. 198a.

corrected certain of them by replacing them with dashes (Ex. 198b).

Ex. 198b.

Nottebohm writes in his *Beethoveniana*

> From these corrections and the letter it appears that Beethoven, at least from 1813 on, placed value of the differ-

entiation of dots and dashes. Equally authentic evidence that this was already the case earlier has not yet come to light. If one may judge by a few old editions, it is beyond doubt that Beethoven distinguished between the signs already in 1800.[63]

One modern edition which reproduces both dashes and dots, the *Vienna Urtext,* differs however from the *staccato* indications in even the few examples given in Nottebohm. Moreover, the evidence regarding Beethoven's usage, according to the *Vienna Urtext,* suggests the opposite of Nottebohm's conclusion, since all instances of the presence of both marks are found in sonatas written before 1813.

In a recent study published by the Beethoven House, Paul Mies concludes that, although Beethoven intended a difference in the degree of *staccato,* he was not precise or consistent in his use of the two signs, the dash and the dot. After inspecting over eighty manuscripts, Mies came to the realization that Beethoven apparently wrote what he heard in his mind, and that, as a consequence, *staccato* marks vary from dots to elongated dots to dashes of varying length. As an example he cites the third variation of the first movement of Op. 26, in which the *staccato* marks over the left-hand chords become progressively longer as the intensity grows.[64]

As Clementi wrote in his *Introduction,* the nice degree of more and less depends upon the "character and passion" of the piece. It was this concise handbook which Beethoven chose for his young student, Gerhard von Breuning.

# Notes and Sources

## Chapter IV

[1] Adolf Bernhard Marx, *Anleitung zum Vortrag Beethovenscher Klavierwerke* (Berlin, 1875), p. 48.

[2] Anton Schindler, *Beethoven as I Knew Him,* edited by Donald W. MacArdle (Chapel Hill: The University of North Carolina Press, 1966), p. 417.

[3] Anton Schindler, *Für Studirende von Beethoven's Clavier-Musik* (in *Niederrheinische Musik-Zeitung,* 1853-1867), No. 45, pp. 156-157.

[4] Carl Philipp Emanuel Bach, *Essay on the True Art of Playing Keyboard Instruments,* translated and edited by William J. Mitchell (New York: W. W. Norton, 1949), p. 153.

[5] Schindler, *Beethoven as I Knew Him,* pp. 417-420, 497-501.

[6] *Ibid.,* p. 417.

[7] Schindler, *Für Studirende,* p. 157.

[8] Anna Gertrud Huber, *Beethovens Anmerkungen zu einer Auswahl von Cramer-Etuden* (Zurich: Hug & Company, 1961), p. 3.

[9] *Ibid.,* p. 5.

[10] Schindler, *Für Studirende,* p. 157.

[11] Carl Czerny, *Complete Theoretical and Practical Piano Forte School* (London, 1839), Vol. III, p. 6.

[12] *Ibid.,* p. 7.

[13] Schindler, *Beethoven as I Knew Him,* p. 416.

[14] Czerny, *Piano Forte School,* Vol. III, p. 8.

[15] Carl Czerny, *Vollständige theoretisch-practische Pianoforte-Schule, Op. 500* (Vienna, 1842), Vol. IV, p. 42.

[16] Czerny, *Piano Forte School,* Vol. III, p. 9.

[17] *Ibid.,* p. 100.

[18] *Ibid.,* p. 10.

[19] Czerny, *Pianoforte-Schule,* Vol. IV, p. 39.

[20] *Ibid.,* p. 51.

[21] Czerny, *Piano Forte School,* Vol. III, p. 11.

[22] Czerny, *Pianoforte-Schule,* Vol. IV, p. 64.

[23]Czerny, *Piano Forte School,* Vol. III, p. 12.

[24]Czerny, *Pianoforte-Schule,* Vol. IV, p. 39.

[25]*Ibid.,* p. 50.

[26]Marx, *Anleitung,* p. 54.

[27]*Ibid.*

[28]*Ibid.*

[29]Czerny, *Pianoforte-Schule,* Vol. IV, p. 53.

[30]*Ibid.,* p. 63.

[31]*Ibid.,* p. 106-107.

[32]*Ibid.,* p. 111.

[33]Donald Francis Tovey and Harold Craxton (ed.), *Beethoven Sonatas* (London: Associated Board of the Royal Schools of Music, 1931), Vol. II, p. 124.

[34]Czerny, *Pianoforte-Schule,* Vol. IV, p. 52.

[35]Bach, *Essay,* p. 155.

[36]Daniel Gottlob Türk, *Klavierschule* (Leipzig und Halle, 1789), p. 356.

[37]Bach, *Essay,* p. 154.

[38]As an example of the subtlety of touch which Beethoven attempted to indicate, the slurring of the following figure from the first movement of Op. 101 ♪♪♪ implies:

1) that the first note is the heaviest of the three and may be somewhat lengthened;

2) that the finger must be lifted from the second eighth;

3) that the third eighth, although it is detached from and played shorter and lighter than the second eighth, remains part of the three-note figure and must not be regarded as an upbeat to the following beat.

[39]Czerny, *Pianoforte-Schule,* Vol. IV, p. 36.

[40]*Ibid.,* p. 37.

[41]*Ibid.*

[42]*Ibid.*

[43]*Ibid.,* p. 49.

[44]*Thayer's Life of Beethoven,* revised and edited by Elliot Forbes (Princeton: Princeton University Press, 1967; Princeton Paperback, 1970), Vol. I, p. 88.

[45]Anna Gertrud Huber, *Ludwig van Beethoven, Seine Schüler und Interpreten* (Vienna: Walter Krieg, 1953), p. 20.

[46]*Ibid.,* p. 12.

[47]Harold Schonberg, *The Great Pianists* (New York: Simon and

Schuster, 1963), p. 76.

[48]Czerny, *Piano Forte School,* Vol. III, p. 22.

[49]*Ibid.,* p. 19.

[50]*Ibid.,* p. 21.

[51]Czerny, *Pianoforte-Schule,* Vol. IV, p. 45.

[52]*Ibid.,* p. 48.

[53]*Ibid.,* p. 49-50.

[54]*Ibid.,* p. 62.

[55]*Ibid.,* p. 67.

[56]Czerny, *Piano Forte School,* Vol. III, pp. 26-27.

[57]Czerny, *Pianoforte-Schule,* Vol. IV, p. 37.

[58]*Ibid.,* p. 56.

[59]Gustav Nottebohm, *Beethoveniana* (Leipzig and Winterthur, 1872), p. 109.

[60]Muzio Clementi, *Introduction to the Art of Playing the Pianoforte.*

[61]Czerny, *Piano Forte School,* Vol. III, p. 28.

[62]Emily Anderson, *The Letters of Beethoven* (New York: St. Martin's Press, 1961; London: Macmillan & Co.), Vol. III, p. 1242.

[63]Nottebohm, p. 109.

[64]Paul Mies, *Textkritische Untersuchungen bei Beethoven* (Bonn: Beethoven House, 1957), pp. 85-86.

# V

## Pedaling

BEETHOVEN'S use of the pedal has always been a source of dispute. To the ears of the Hummelites, his pedaling "produced only a confused noise."[1] Important changes were taking shape in piano design and construction during the first half of the nineteenth century, and, as the instrument gained in sustaining qualities, adjustments to Beethoven's pedal indications seemed increasingly desirable. Of those who studied with Beethoven, Schindler, who protested his loyalty to Beethoven's instruction so ardently in other respects, had little interest in either fostering an understanding of Beethoven's pedal effects or in discussing the sensuousness of piano tone. In contrast, in the directions for pedaling in the *Piano School* (Vol. IV, Chap. 2), Czerny reports that Beethoven used the pedal much more than is indicated in his scores.[2]

Before selecting these directions of Czerny to learn what Beethoven emphasized, it would be helpful to begin with the best source of information about Beethoven's pedaling — his own scores. A study of Beethoven's pedal markings in his scores reveals a wide range of desired results: *legato,* even gradations of *crescendo* and *diminuendo,* fullness of sound, heightened contrast of dynamic levels, an "impressionistic" play with the qualities of sound, and, to a lesser degree, the connecting of movements by sustained pedal.

**Legato.** — Mention has already been made of Beethoven's dislike for *non legato,* the "Fingertanz" of the preceding generation. As described earlier in the section dealing with *legato,* Beethoven recommended practice holding down successive notes of a melody or passage beyond their notated length to produce a more believable *legato.* However, even such "super-connection" with the fingers as that involved in Beethoven's sustained style can have little effect on an instrument of limited sustaining capacity. Beethoven's use of long pedals promotes a *legato* by permitting sympathetic vibration from undamped strings and by producing a "blur of sound" in which the notes overlap. Thus Schindler explains that the *senza sordini* marking of the *Adagio* of Op. 27/2 was intended to produce a super-legato.[3]

The following examples illustrate this use of the pedal to promote *legato.* In Op. 101, II, a long pedal is accompanied by the indication *sempre legato;* it is significant that the melody lies in the treble, the least sonorous register of Beethoven's piano (Ex. 199).

Ex. 199. Op. 101, II, 30-34

The long pedals in the middle section of the Scherzo of Op. 106 may have been prescribed because of the slurred octave melody over relatively long stretches of harmonic immobility (Ex. 200).

Ex. 200. Op. 106, II, 46-55

**Even Gradations of Crescendo and Diminuendo.** — In the transition from the second *Arioso* to the fugue in inversion in Op. 110, a *crescendo* and *diminuendo* occur under one pedal (Ex. 201). An-

Ex. 201. Op. 110, III, 131-136

other example is found in the recitative which opens the movement; the *Bebung* device would not be successful without the pedal (Ex. 202).

Ex. 202. Op. 110, III, 4-6

A *diminuendo* under a long pedal occurs in the same movement at the transition from the fugue to the second *Arioso*. Since the sonority of the modern piano presents the pianist with more tone than he wants to retain in a passage such as this, it is more often than not the case to arrive at the *piano* in measure 113 with too much sound left over. It is therefore important to notice that Beethoven directs that the *diminuendo* begin immediately (Ex. 203). A long

Ex. 203. Op. 110, III, 110-115

pedal frequently accompanied a *diminuendo* at the end of a movement or a section (Exx. 204, 205). The final movement of this

Ex. 204. Op. 26, I, 213-219

Ex. 205. Op. 26, III, 72-75

sonata also ends quietly under a long pedal. In fact, this is the first
sonata in which Beethoven left any pedal indications. The pedal was
also used to cover a *diminuendo* at the end of a section (Exx. 206,

Ex. 206. Op. 28, I, 251-257

207). A long pedal may blur two different harmonies or neighboring
pitches under a pedaled *diminuendo* (Exx. 208, 209).

Ex. 207. Op. 53, III, 378-402

Ex. 208. Op. 53, III, 97-101

Ex. 209. Op. 57, I, 233-238

The pedal helped to produce a *crescendo* in some instances (Exx. 210, 211).

Ex. 210. Op. 106, I, 402-405

Ex. 211. Op. 111, I, 1-2

In other instances, the long pedal enabled the player to accumulate sound much as he would have done whether Beethoven had so indicated the pedal or not (Exx. 212, 213). The pedal and the in-

Ex. 212. Op. 78, II, 175-177

Ex. 213. Op. 111, II, 102-105

creased rhythmic activity in both hands are contributing factors in creating the *crescendo* near the end of the third movement of Op. 106 (Ex. 214).

Ex. 214. Op. 106, III, 163-165

**Fullness of Sound.** — In utilizing a long pedal in the opening of the first movement of Op. 106, Beethoven augments the *fortissimo* over the sustained B-flat major harmony (Ex. 215). The finale of the

Ex. 215. Op. 106, I, 1-4

"Appassionata" also opens with a long pedal over a hammered diminished-seventh chord (Ex. 216). In measure 37-44 of Op. 81a,

Ex. 216. Op. 57, III, 1-6

as in the opening of Op. 106, the presence of the long pedal shows that the *staccato* marks are touch indications determining a quality of sound rather than the length of the notes (Ex. 217). A long pedal

Ex. 217. Op. 81a, III, 37-44

is used for fullness of sound both in *fortissimo* endings of movements (Op. 53, III; Op. 57, III; Op. 81a, III; Op. 110, III) and in *pianissimo* endings (Op. 57, I; Op. 106, III; Op. 110, II; Op. 111, I).

The pedal was also used with single *fortissimo* or *sforzando* chords (Ex. 218).

Ex. 218. Op. 106, I, 323-325

**Heightened Contrast of Dynamic Levels.** — The pedal adds the resonance of undamped strings to a *forte* or *fortissimo*. It is assumed that a *piano* which alternates with a *forte* is pedaled in a normal fashion (Ex. 219). The release of the pedal at the *piano* in this

Ex. 219. Op. 53, III, 221-229

passage suggests that the tone of Beethoven's piano, particularly in the bass, did not fall away as rapidly as one might have expected. Beethoven particularly exploited dynamic contrast through the use of the damper pedal in the middle and late sonatas (Exx. 220, 221, 222). In a passage from the trio of the second movement of Op. 110, the relatively poor quality of the high treble on Beethoven's piano may have been disguised by the ring produced in the piano with undamped strings. (Ex. 223).

Ex. 220. Op. 53, III, 441-445

Ex. 221. Op. 78, II, 57-61

Ex. 222. Op. 106, I, 17-20

Ex. 223. Op. 110, II, 40-48

In the development section of the first movement of Op. 79, Beethoven heightened the contrast of texture by indicating the pedal in the *piano* passage but omitting it in the *forte* passage with its jabbing *sforzandi* (Ex. 224.)

Ex. 224. Op. 79, I, 86-93

**Impressionistic Play with Qualities of Sound.** — The present-day pianist, who is perhaps disturbed most of all by those pedal indications of Beethoven which produce impressionistic sound qualities, usually ascribes such an indication to one of two conditions, Beethoven's hearing or his piano. The blurring of tonic and dominant harmonies at the opening of the Rondo of Op. 53 has been explained as an instance of the use of the split damper pedal, the right half of which raised the treble dampers and the left those in the bass. According to this explanation, Beethoven wanted to have only the low C (or G, as the case may be) sounding through. Beethoven, however, made a note on the margin of the first page of the manuscript, which indicated that, at the sign *Ped,* all dampers — bass and treble — were to be raised. Even had he not given these specific directions, it is likely that the left side of the split damper pedal would have controlled at least that part of the broken chord figure in the right hand which lies below middle C. In addition to the repetitions of the theme, there are other passages of an impressionistic type in the same movement (Ex. 225). At one point in the manu-

Ex. 225. Op. 53, III, 251-254

script, Beethoven used a red crayon to replace a quarter rest with two eighth rests in order to show that the pedal was to be released with the second eighth rest (Ex. 226).

Ex. 226. Op. 53, III, 106-113

In a passage from the development section of the first movement of Op. 106, the imitation of horns is made to sound, by means of the pedal, as though it were fading away in the distance (Ex. 227).

Ex. 227. Op. 106, I, 132-138

Beethoven reportedly said that the recitatives in the first movement of Op. 31/2 should sound like a voice from within a vault (Ex. 228).[4]

Ex. 228. Op. 31/2, I, 143-148

**Connecting Movements.** — To maintain the character of a work from one movement to the next, the pedal is used to prevent any interruption of sound (Exx. 229, 230).

Ex. 229. Op. 27/1, I-II, 84-4

Ex. 230. Op. 109, I-II, 97-4

Czerny's comments on pedal usage in the Sonatas presumably reflect Beethoven's own practice and the directions given his students. The validity of the pedaling which he suggests is supported by his faithfulness in retaining Beethoven's original pedal markings — in contrast with Moscheles. The additional pedalings which

Czerny recommends principally reinforce Beethoven's objectives of continuity and fullness of sound. Czerny repeatedly refers to such pedaling as *harmonios*: "With the word *harmonios* we denote preferably a correct use of the pedal through the duration of consonant harmony."[5]

At the transition to A-flat major (at the end before the cadenza) the pedal is to be used *harmonios*.[6] [Ex. 231.]

Ex. 231. Op. 2/3, I, 217-232

The *Trio legato* and *harmonios*. The first note in the third measure extremely strong, and with pedal, which then can last two measures.[7] [Ex. 232.]

Ex. 232. Op. 7, III, Trio

Moscheles gives an identical pedaling in his edition for the opening of the Trio of Op. 7, III. Both he and Czerny intend the same pattern to be continued throughout the section.

Of the *Adagio* of Op. 31/2, Czerny states: "The pedal must contribute in the proper places to the sustaining of the harmonies."[8] Moscheles' only pedalings in this movement apply to the "tympani" figure (Ex. 233).

Ex. 233. Op. 31/2, II, 17-22. *According to Moscheles*

Czerny wrote of the opening of Op. 31/2, III:

The right hand always lightly broken off, the left as *legato* as possible. The 6 sixteenths — which are divided between the hands must follow upon one another as evenly as possible, in order, as it were, to suggest the gallop of a horse. This movement lasts through the whole piece and is enlivened only through an exact observance of the *piano,* the *forte, crescendo, diminuendo,* and also through the use of the pedal in passages of consonant harmony (Ex. 234).[9]

Ex. 234. Op. 31/2, III, 1-11. *Accoring to Czerny and Moscheles*

Czerny studied this sonata with Beethoven; Moscheles in all probability heard Beethoven or one of his students play it. Since both agree about the pedaling of the opening measures, it is difficult to doubt that this was Beethoven's intention. If Beethoven had objected to this pedaling, Czerny would hardly have recommended it. One gathers from Czerny's comments that evenness was uppermost in his mind, and this because of the character of the piece and the imagery which we are told originated with Beethoven.

Czerny refers to measures 50-56 from Op. 53, I, as "brilliant and *harmonios,* with use of the pedal" (Ex. 235).[10]

Ex. 235. Op. 53, I, 50-55

The following two comments of Czerny are given without examples since the particular passages have been quoted earlier. Czerny says of the Scherzo of Op. 106:

> The *Trio* (B-flat minor) harmonios *legato* and always with good use of the pedal.[11] [Ex. 214.]

And of the second movement of Op. 110:

> The *Trio* (D-flat major) softly, fluently, and *harmonisch* by means of the *pedal.*[12] [Ex. 223.]

There are other examples given by Czerny involving static harmony.

> In the 11th measure of the second section the pedal is to be used during the cross-over of the left hand, so long as the harmony does not change.[13] [Ex. 236.]

Moscheles' pedaling here is identical.

Ex. 236. Op. 2/2, I, 133-143

The *pedal* is very practicable with the [left hand] cross-over before the return of the main theme.[14] [Ex. 237.]

Ex. 237. Op. 31/1, I, 170-178

Moscheles indicates no pedal and, in fact, adds *staccato* dashes to the left-hand quarter notes.

The use of the pedal in Examples 236 and 237, as well as in Ex. 238, is related to the desire for greater smoothness and *legato,* for "in music, the Legato is the rule, and all other modes of execution are only the exceptions."[15]

The pedal can be depressed for a moment each time with the bass notes before the [left hand] cross-over.[16]

Ex. 238. Op. 2/3, II, 19-21

To achieve greater fullness of sound in certain passages, Czerny advises a pedal of appropriate length. At the end of the exposition of Op. 13, I, he states:

> In the last 8 measures of the first part each measure with *pedal*.[17] [Ex. 239.]

Ex. 239. Op. 13, I, 125-132

In the first movement of Op. 31/2 he indicates that:

> From the 21st measure, *pedal* up to the *piano,* and the same with each *forte* of this section up to measure 41.[18] [Ex. 240.]

Ex. 240. Op. 31/2, I, 21-29

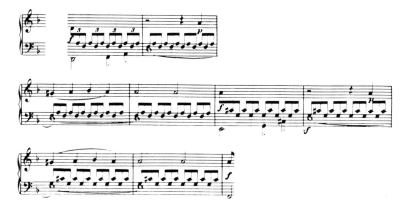

Moscheles' pedaling in this passage places all four measures, including the *forte* and the *piano,* under the same pedal. Considering the blurring that this produces, it is difficult to understand why Moscheles found Beethoven's long pedals in the "Waldstein" objectionable.

Czerny speaks of the use of the pedal in strong, harmonic passages:

> ... the role played by the *pedal* is not to be overlooked in all

consonant, powerful places, as for example measures 14, 17, 20, etc.[19] [Ex. 241.]

Ex. 241. Op. 57, I, 13-24

The importance of the pedal in producing a *crescendo* is revealed in Czerny's remarks on performing the Thirty-Two Variations.

> Above all, the *crescendo* to *fortissimo* in variations 31 and 32 is to be attended to by any and all means, especially by means of the *pedal*.[20]

Both Czerny and Moscheles concur in their pedaling with the *diminuendo* at the close of the following two movements:

> Op. 7, IV. "The end of the *Rondo* very light, always softer, and quietly fading away, the last 4 measures with *pedal*."[21]

> Op. 10/1, II. "At the end, dying away quietly, with both pedals."[22]

Czerny comments on Beethoven's impressionistic pedalings in the "Waldstein" that:

> This *Rondo,* of a pastoral *character,* is entirely calculated on the use of the pedal, which here [the opening is quoted in Czerny's text] seems essential.[23]

Czerny and Moscheles both indicate a pedaling of an impression-istic type in measures 155-158 of the fourth movement of Op. 7 (Ex. 242). Czerny writes:

> The *pedal* is to be depressed precisely with the first B♮ octave and held down continuously for 2½ measures.[24]

Ex. 242. Op. 7, IV, 154-158

Schindler, who left no directions regarding pedaling in his teacher's works, accused Czerny of an "indiscriminate use" of the pedal.[25] On the contrary, one who used the pedal indiscriminately would not likely be concerned about the symbols used to indicate the exact point at which the pedal is to be depressed and released — as Czerny was:

> It is known that many composers, instead of the word *Ped.*, for the sake of brevity, place the sign ⊕ where it is to be depressed and the sign ✳ where it is to be released. This way is also better, because it is more precise.[26]

Far less precise than *Ped.* ✳ is *senza sordini* (without dampers, that is, with pedal), the phrase which Beethoven used in Op. 26, Op. 27/1, and Op. 27/2 to indicate the use of of pedal. According to Czerny, "the indication *senza Sordino* was used only so long as one still controlled the dampers with a knee pedal."[27] The pedal lyre as we know it was an invention of Broadwood in 1783; it was adopted by Erard the same year and by Stein in 1789.[28] Although this precedes by ten to fifteen years Beethoven's use of the indication *senza sordini,* it is not difficult to imagine that many pianos with the old knee-pedal mechanism would still have been in use into the first decade of the nineteenth century. Although *senza sordini* alone may have been equivalent to *con Pedale* — the pedal

to be changed at intervals but never raised for any length of time —
the indication for the release of the pedal after *senza sordini* is *con
sordini,* literally "with dampers."

Although it is certain that Beethoven used the *una corda* frequently, it is indicated only in Op. 101, Op. 106, Op. 109 and Op.
110. The *Verschiebung* (the German term for the shifting of the
action) of Beethoven's piano was designed to move the hammer in a
position to strike two strings as well as only one. Thus Beethoven
could direct, in Op. 101, III, *Nach und nach mehrere Saiten* ("Little
by little more strings") (Ex. 243). The *una corda* effect was far

Ex. 243. Op. 101, III, 19-20

more noticeable on pianos of Beethoven's day than on present-day
pianos which do not go beyond *due corde.* Consequently, the decision of precisely where to use an *una corda* is more important when
playing on an old instrument than when using a modern piano.

Czerny refers to the use of this pedal in six sonatas other than
the ones previously indicated. He recommends the *una corda* in the
Rondo of Op. 7 at the modulation to E major after the last *fermata*
on the B-flat octaves (Ex. 242)[29] and in the last twenty-two measures of the Adagio of Op. 10/1.[30] Czerny indicates that Beethoven
used the *una corda* throughout the *Adagio* of Op. 27/2 except
during the *crescendo-forte-descrescendo* in the middle section of the
movement.[31] Czerny recommends the *una corda* in all sections
marked *pianissimo* in the Rondo of the "Waldstein,"[32] and in the
first movement of Op. 81a throughout the section where tonic and
dominant harmonies are superimposed (Ex. 244).[33]

Ex. 244. Op. 81a, I, 223-235

Of the slow movement of Op. 57 Czerny wrote:

The second *variation* pp and with *Verschiebung,* very *legato, cantabile* and very expressively.

The third *variation* without *pedal* . . . [34]

Paul Badura-Skoda suggests that "without pedal" in this case does not refer to the damper pedal but instead to the *Verschiebung,* which Czerny had indicated in the previous variation.[35]

**Summary.** — Beethoven was an untiring developer, not just in the transformation of motivic patterns, but in the exploitation of all possible expressive means as well. Faced with a piano that was still in the adolescent years of its development, Beethoven used the pedal to fill in holes in the sound, to augment contrasts in dynamics, to help the instrument "sing," and to explore the spectrum of shading it afforded.

Beethoven, therefore, did not hear a pre-packaged sound. What he heard in his imagination was more colorful and grandiose than his piano could produce. Unfortunately the reverse is often true of us.

Complaints about Beethoven's long (damper) pedals were already voiced by his contemporaries, who of course heard the blurring in relation to the sonority of their piano. In the sonatas, the only such passage which is difficult to manage occurs in the Rondo of the *Waldstein.* The degree of appreciable blurring on a large modern grand in a recital hall would be comparable to that experienced by Beethoven's contemporaries on their instruments. That which Beethoven heard in his imagination was the inner "must" which determined the indications on the written page. These should be precisely followed. In order to do so, it is the responsibility of the performer to develop a sensitivity of touch to control the level of blur.

# Notes and Sources

## Chapter V

[1]O. G. Sonneck, *Beethoven: Impressions by his Contemporaries* (New York: Dover Publications, 1967), p. 29. Reprinted through permission of the publisher.

[2]*Thayer's Life of Beethoven,* revised and edited by Elliot Forbes (Princeton: Princeton University Press, 1967; Princeton Paperback, 1970), Vol. I, p. 368.

[3]Anton Schindler, *Beethoven as I Knew Him,* edited by Donald W. MacArdle (Chapel Hill: The University of North Carolina Press, 1966), p. 422.

[4]Donald Francis Tovey and Harold Craxton (ed.), *Beethoven Sonatas* (London: Associated Board of the Royal Schools of Music, 1931), Vol. II, p. 125.

[5]Carl Czerny, *Vollständige theoretisch-practische Pianoforte-Schule, Op. 500* (Vienna, 1842), Vol. IV, p. 115.

[6]*Ibid.,* p. 38.

[7]*Ibid.,* p. 40.

[8]*Ibid.,* p. 56.

[9]*Ibid.*

[10]*Ibid.,* p. 58.

[11]*Ibid.,* p. 66.

[12]*Ibid.,* p. 68.

[13]*Ibid.,* p. 36.

[14]*Ibid.,* p. 54.

[15]Carl Czerny, *Complete Theoretical and Practical Piano Forte School* (London, 1839), Vol. III, p. 22.

[16]Czerny, *Pianoforte-Schule,* Vol. IV, p. 39.

[17]*Ibid.,* p. 45.

[18]*Ibid.,* p. 55.

[19]*Ibid.,* p. 61.

[20]*Ibid.,* p. 72.

[21]*Ibid.,* p. 41.

[22]*Ibid.,* p. 42.

[23]*Ibid.,* p. 59.

[24]*Ibid.,* p. 41.

[25]Schindler, p. 145.

[26]Czerny, *Pianoforte-Schule,* Vol. IV, p. 50.

[27]*Ibid.,* p. 59.

[28]Ernest Closson, *History of the Piano* (London: Paul Elek, 1947), p. 87.

[29]Czerny, *Pianoforte-Schule,* Vol. IV, p. 41.

[30]*Ibid.,* p. 42.

[31]*Ibid.,* p. 51.

[32]*Ibid.,* p. 59.

[33]*Ibid.,* p. 63.

[34]*Ibid.,* p. 61.

[35]Carl Czerny, *Ueber den richtigen Vortrag der Sämtlichen Beethoven'schen Klavierwerke* (Vienna: Universal Edition, 1963), p. 5.

# VI

# *Ornamentation*

THE ORNAMENTS found in the Beethoven sonatas include trills, turns, trilled turns (*Prallender Doppelschlag*), appoggiaturas and arpeggiated chords. In addition to the scanty information given by Beethoven himself for the performance of the trills in the Rondo of the "Waldstein," there are three sources which may be consulted regarding ornaments generally in Beethoven: the Bach *Essay* (which Czerny used when studying with Beethoven), the Czerny *Piano School* (which contains, besides a section devoted to ornaments, the important chapter dealing with the performance of Beethoven's piano works), and the Clementi *Introduction to the Art of Playing the Pianoforte* (which Beethoven procured in a German translation for Gerhard von Breuning).

**Trills.** — In the autograph of the "Waldstein," Beethoven gave directions for the performance of the long trills in the *Prestissimo* of the Rondo (Exx. 245a, b, c). In it he answers questions about the starting note and fullness of the trill, although one should not immediately assume that these directions apply to all trills in Beethoven.

Ex. 245a. Op. 53, III, 485-492

N. B. Those for whom the trill is too difficult, here where the theme is joined with it, may facilitate the trill in the following manner [Ex. 245b], or, according to the extent of their capacity, also double it [Ex. 245c].

Ex. 245b.

Ex. 245c.

Of these sextuplets two are played to each quarter in the bass. Generally it is not important if this trill also loses something of its usual speed.[1]

The crossed-out G-natural at the beginning of each measure in Beethoven's first example (Ex. 245b), as well as the shade of the ink and the slant of the handwriting, suggests that Beethoven automatically thought of the trill beginning on the main note. Thinking that the performer would also begin the trills throughout the movement on the main note, he placed the upper note in the form of an appoggiatura before each long trill in the movement (with the exception of measure 497). The fact that the first melody note, G, lies an octave above the trilled note reinforces the natural inclination to begin the trill on the main note.

If one includes as an original direction for the performance of trills those trills which Beethoven wrote out in full in other sonatas, a preference for beginning the trill on the main note seems to be stronger. In the Rondo of Op. 90 there is such a trill, beginning on the principal note, which becomes a double trill in contrary motion in measure 48, probably for the sake of sonority (Ex. 246). In

Ex. 246a. Op. 90, II, 40-42

Ex. 246b. Op. 90, II, 48-52

Variation VI of the last movement of Op. 109 a similarly written trill begins on the principal note in both hands, increases to thirty-second notes and ultimately turns into an unmeasured trill (Ex. 247). It seems likely that Beethoven would have gone into the trill smoothly — from the principal note, as in the preceding measures. Here the number of notes in the indicated trill would be important, since, to continue the pattern of acceleration, the trill notes would have to be faster than the preceding thirty-seconds. Another written

Ex. 247a. Op. 109, III, 159-161

Ex. 247b. Op. 109, III, 164-165

trill beginning on the principal note is found at the transition from the *Maestoso* to the *Allegro* of the first movement of Op. 111 (Ex.

Ex. 248. Op. 111, I, 15-16

248). The difficult double trill in the second movement of the same sonata was fingered by Beethoven to begin on the auxiliary notes, possibly for the reason that it is easier to play this way (Ex. 249).

Ex. 249. Op. 111, II, 112-113

In measure 160 of the second movement of Op. 54, Beethoven would hardly have repeated the auxiliary note C-natural in the trill (Ex. 250).

Ex. 250. Op. 54, II, 158-161

In the section dealing with ornaments in the *Piano School,* Czerny indicates that a trill may begin in one of three ways. It may begin with the principal note:

> This occurs when prior to the shake, either nothing has preceded, or some other note, not the same as the principal note, and which therefore must be taken on another key.

or with the auxiliary note:

> This must always be the case when the principal note of the shake immediately precedes the commencement of it.

or with the lower of the concluding notes.[2]

According to this advice from Czerny, the trills over the quarter notes in the *Menuetto* of Op. 2/1 should begin with the auxiliary note since the main note of the trill is preceded each time but one by the same note. In the interest of uniformity, the first trill should perhaps also begin on the auxiliary note (Ex. 251). Beethoven's

Ex. 251. Op. 2/1, III, 28-36

use of an appoggiatura preceding the trill in measure 78 of Op. 2/3, I, supports Czerny's rule (Ex. 252). According to this rule also,

Ex. 252. Op. 2/3, I, 77-79

all trills in the first movement of Op. 57 which do not start from below would begin with the upper auxiliary (Ex. 253).

Ex. 253. Op. 57, I, 9-12

In those instances where there is insufficient time for more than four notes in a trill, a turn should be used instead of a trill, according to the Bach *Essay*.[3] A turn could, therefore, be used instead of a trill in each of the following passages (Exx. 254-256).

Ex. 254. Op. 2/1, IV, 9-12. *Prestissimo*

Ex. 255. Op. 2/3, I, 59-60

Ex. 256. Op. 2/3, IV, 23-25

The *Pralltriller* ⟊ or half-trill, as described by Bach,[4] consists of four notes ♩ ♪♪♪♪. to be played very rapidly — so rapidly, in fact, that the individual notes will not be easily distinguished. In a descending figure ♪♪♪ played in a quick tempo, the four-note pattern ♪♪♪♪ of the trill becomes in actuality: ♪♪♪ . As such, the ornament then fits Bach's subsequent description of the *Schneller,* or snap, although Bach notates the latter ♪♪ and indicates that it is only used before short, detached notes. Marpurg's explanation, given in his *Anleitung zum Clavierspielen* (1756), reveals the confusion of nomenclature surrounding the two ornaments which in practice were often indistinguishable from each other:

(2) If the tied note of a simple enclosed trill is omitted and the ornament, contrary to the rule, begins at once with

the main note, the trill is shortened and limited to *three notes*: the result is of course an incomplete trill which is, however, in certain instances more suitable than the regular complete trill. These instances consist of stepwise descending passages in *rapid tempo* . . . a short note preceded by a long appoggiatura . . . or . . . a note which is shortened by an appoggiatura . . . Herr Bach calls this trill a *Pralltriller* because of the speed with which these three notes, and no more, must be executed; he further observes that, if this ornament occurs over a fermata, one holds the appoggiatura quite long and thereafter snaps off very abruptly with this trill, in the course of which one lifts the finger from the key very quickly.

(3) If one wishes to use the *Pralltriller* suddenly on one note, both notes (of which the trill consists) preceding the main note must be notated either in small notes or the same size as the other notes . . . Herr Bach calls this ornament a *Schneller*. It will be seen that this ornament — whether it is indicated with notes or notated as an abbreviated enclosed trill and called a *Pralltriller* — is none other than a short inverted mordent . . . Nevertheless, one must never call the *Schneller* a mordent, as some clavecinists foolishly do. One must always refer to each ornament with its correct name.[5]

In his *Klavierschule* Türk comments on what he considers the improper notation of the *Schneller*:

One notices that, in examples c), d) and e)

Ex. 256a.

which I have borrowed from the works of Bach, E. W. Wolf and others, the Pralltriller has been mistakenly used instead of the Schneller which belong here.[6]

Finally, Clementi, in his *Introduction to the Art of Playing the Pianoforte,* refers to the *Pralltriller* as a "transient" or "passing" shake and gives as an example:                      With

respect to trills in general, Clementi continues: ". . . composers trust
CHIEFLY to the taste and judgment of the performer, whether it
shall be long, short, transient, or turned."[7]

In Op. 2/3, I, mentioned above (Ex. 225), not only would the
*Schneller* or snap be less crowded than a full *Pralltriller*, it would also
seem preferable from a melodic standpoint, since in each case (meas.
56-60) the note which begins the phrase is the main note of the
*Pralltriller*. In Op. 7, I, measure 108-109, a snap could also be
used. (Ex. 257). Of the *Pralltriller*, really a *Schneller*, in the finale

Ex. 257. Op. 7, I, 108-111

of Op. 31/2 (Ex. 258a) Czerny writes:

Ex. 258a. Op. 31/2, III, 43-45

The Pralltriller are executed as follows [Ex. 258b]:

Ex. 258b.

in that the main note must be strongly emphasized after the
two small notes.[8]

By playing the small notes as quickly as Czerny directs and by
placing the accent on the third note, the *Schneller* sounds as though
it had been played ahead of the beat, which, it may be assumed,
Czerny intended.

According to Bach, in a situation where a short trill would be
crowded, a short appoggiatura may be used (Ex. 259).[9]

Ex. 259a. Op. 22, I, 9-10

Ex. 259b.

As for the question of whether a turn should be used at the end of a trill, Czerny simply says that the turn must be added if the composer has not written it. According to Czerny, the turn is omitted only in chain trills, although it may be added if the chain ascends.[10]

**Turns.** — Beethoven left no specific directions for playing the turn. However, if he followed Bach's instructions and if Czerny — in those few instances in which he refers to the turn — correctly reflects Beethoven's ideas, some conclusions about his preferences may be formed.

According to Bach, the turn is a miniature trill with a turn,[11] differing from the trill in that the final notes of the turn are not played as quickly as the beginning notes. Also, according to Bach, the turn is sometimes played broadly in a slow movement.[12] Czerny makes no mention of the rhythmic spacing of the notes of a turn, saying only that a turn between two notes "must be introduced as late as possible, namely, just before the following note."[13] The turn in measure 111 in the finale of Op. 2/1 should probably be played on the fourth beat (Ex. 260). The turn in measure 34 of Op. 10/1,

Ex. 260. Op. 2/1, IV, 111-113

II, is notated by Beethoven to be played "as late as possible" (Ex. 261a), while the trill seven measures later must also be played as

Ex. 261a. Op. 10/1, II, 34-35

an extremely quick turn (Ex. 261b). The written turns in measure

Ex. 261b. Op. 10/1, II, 40-42

53 of Op. 10/3, II, and in measure 4 of the last movement of the same sonata, follow Bach's description of the final notes differing rhythmically from those which precede them (Exx. 262, 263).

Ex. 262. Op. 10/3, II, 52-53

Ex. 263. Op. 10/3, IV, 2-4

The opening measures of Op. 2/1, II, provide an illustration of Bach's statement that in a slow movement a turn may be played broadly. If the turn in this example were to be played quickly and as late as possible, the appoggiatura which follows it would be absorbed into the end of the turn and thereby lose its own identity (Ex. 264).

Ex. 264. Op. 2/1, II, 1-2

In the first movement of Op. 31/2 Czerny's use of an F-double-sharp instead of an F-sharp for the lowest note of the turn (as it is found in the *Gesamtausgabe,* as well as in modern Urtext editions) relates the turn to the motivic fragments set in a turn-like pattern in the same movement (Ex. 265).[14] In view of this, a broad execution of the turn helps to reveal its motivic significance.

Ex. 265. Op. 31/2, I, 6, 22-24, 55-59

**Trilled Turn.** — Bach differentiated between the trilled turn (  ), which occurs in a descending second, and the snapped turn, which is formed by prefixing a note of the same pitch to a turn over a detached note.[15] Both figures sound as though begun on the principal note; the difference between the two is rhythmic rather than melodic. The trilled turn in measure 17 of Op. 78, I, (Ex. 266), is given as a simple turn in the *Gesamtausgabe* but as a trilled turn in modern Urtext editions.

Ex. 266. Op. 78, I, 16-17

The trilled turn in this example could be played as follows:

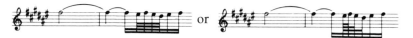

Two instances of the snapped turn occur in measures 20 and 24 of Op. 54, I (Ex. 267). Again, the *Gesamtausgabe* gives only a simple turn.

Ex. 267. Op. 54, I, 20-24

Here the snapped turn could be played:

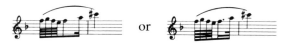

In a statement of the same phrase a few measures earlier, Beethoven has indicated a trill over the E-natural: (Ex. 268).

Ex. 268. Op. 54, I, 12-16

which might be realized in this manner:

Such a realization prevents confusion with either a trilled or snapped turn. Rhythmically this realization fits the dotted rhythm of its phrase just as Beethoven's own realization further on into the movement fits the rhythm of its phrase (Ex. 269).

Ex. 269. Op. 54, I, 117-121

Possibly Bach's detailed discussion of the trilled and snapped turns would have interested Beethoven more from the standpoint of a description of variation in a pattern than as a rule of usage to be followed. Thus, the figure in some instances has the melodic outline of a snapped turn, although without the rhythmic snap (Exx. 270, 271).

Ex. 270. Op. 31/1, II, 31

Ex. 271. Op. 109, III, Variation 1

**Appoggiaturas and Arpeggiated Chords.** — The term *appoggiatura,* as it is used here, refers to conventional notation such as the following:

i.e., to all single small notes. Groups of two or three small notes are described as "compound appoggiaturas," a term which seems justi-

fiable in view of the fact that such groups frequently require an excution beginning on the beat. Beethoven wrote both single and
compound appoggiaturas, the latter taking the form of inverted turns,
slides and broken chords. Since compound appoggiaturas in the
form of broken chords are very similar to arpeggiated chords, the
latter may be included with appoggiaturas in general.

The important question with respect to the performance of
appoggiaturas in the works of Beethoven is not so much one of
length as of accent and position in relation to the beat. The comparatively few instances involving a question of length are illustrated
by Examples 272-275. The first four instances are similar, and
according to Türk, the appoggiaturas are short. He writes in his
*Klavierschule*:

> . . . all appoggiaturas are of short duration . . . if the melody
> rises a step and immediately returns to the same pitch.[16]

Ex. 272a. 2/1, III, 10-14

Ex. 272b. Op. 2/1, III, 19-24

Ex. 273. Op. 10/2, II, 5-8

Ex. 274. Op. 10/3, IV, 7-9

53-56

same rule in the *Essay*.[17] Czerny realizes a similar
in the slow movement of the *Trio,* Op. 1/2 (Ex.
276).

Ex. 276. Op. 1/2, II, 3

When an appoggiatura precedes two or more notes which are
to be sounded simultaneously, Czerny indicates precisely the performance practice in the *Piano School*:

> When a simple Appoggiatura of this kind stands before a
> *chord* or a pair of double notes, it belongs only to that note
> which stands close to it. It must therefore be struck simul-
> taneously with all the other notes; and that note which is
> next to it must be struck afterwards.[19]

Fortunately, Czerny clarifies the uncertainty over the length
of the eighth-note appoggiatura in the first movement of Op. 10/3:

> Note that in the following place: [Ex. 275] the little note is
> a long appoggiatura and therefore must be played as an
> eighth:[20]

The most troublesome question with which the pianist must
contend is that of where to play the unvarying, short, single appoggiatura. Should it fall ahead of the beat or on the beat, and if the
latter, should it be accented or unaccented? The following examples
illustrate how the problem is compounded by Beethoven's own
wide range of treatment. The examples are grouped as follows:

1) Fully written out notes which resemble appoggiaturas
played ahead of the beat.

2) Appoggiaturas whose position ahead of the beat seems
to be implied.

3) Appoggiaturas which seem to sound better ahead of the
beat.

4) Figures which resemble an appoggiatura falling on the beat.

5) Appoggiaturas which must be played on the beat.

6) Appoggiaturas which seem to sound better if played on the beat.

7) Appoggiaturas which stand alone, without any accompanying voice against which they may be placed.

*Fully written out notes which resemble appoggiaturas played ahead of the beat.* (Exx. 277, 278).

Ex. 277. Op. 28, II, 23-26

Ex. 278. Op. 31/2, III, 23-28

*Appoggiaturas whose position ahead of the beat seems to be implied.* The appoggiaturas in Op. 2/2, I, seem to belong ahead of the beat for two reasons. First, the triplet anacrusis, which emphasizes the beat so strongly, sets the pattern for the upbeat character of the appoggiatura, and, second, because of this strong rhythmic accent, the eighth-notes in the top voice must fall exactly on their respective beats (Ex. 279).

Ex. 279. Op. 2/2, I, 181-183

Because the single and compound appoggiaturas in measure 15 and the single appoggiaturas in measure 16 of Op. 101, III, result in the main notes in each hand being played together, it would seem consistent to play the appoggiatura in the left hand in measures 12, 13 and 14 ahead of the beat.

Ex. 280. Op. 101, III, 10-16

Appoggiaturas which seem to sound better played ahead of the beat. The presence of a *sforzando* over the main note in some instances strengthens the natural impulse to play the appoggiatura ahead of the beat (Exx. 281-283).

Ex. 281. Op. 2/2, IV, 26-28

Ex. 282. Op. 13, I, 51-55

Ex. 283. Op. 14/2, III, 4-8

Playing the appoggiatura ahead of the beat seems preferable in certain places, possibly because the notes on the beat strongly outline a tonic triad (Exx. 284-285).

Ex. 284. Op. 13, III, 1-4

Ex. 285. Op. 90, II, 28-30

*Figures which resemble an appoggiatura falling on the beat.* The broken octave figure in measures 193-195 from the first movement of Op. 10/2 is actually an appoggiatura with its consequent main note, both written in large notation (Ex. 286).

Ex. 286. Op. 10/2, I, 193-195

*Appoggiaturas which must be played on the beat.* C.P.E. Bach cautions that the final note of a turn must never run directly into a following appoggiatura.[21] In measures 1 and 5 of Op. 2/1, II, the appoggiatura must come exactly on the beat in order to avoid being absorbed in the turn (Ex. 287).

Ex. 287. Op. 2/1, II, 1-2

The quick note preceding the appoggiatura in measures 2-3, 8-9, 9-10, 10-11, 14-15, and 16-17 of the first variation of Op. 109, III, makes it necessary to play the appoggiatura in these measures on the beat (Ex. 288).

Ex. 288. Op. 109, III, Variation 1

*Appoggiaturas which seem to sound better if played on the beat.* In each of the following excerpts, the physical control required to produce the difference in accent between the appoggiatura played on the beat and the main note which follows gives the phrase or the particular group of notes a "placed" or "intended" character. The effect is much like that of *rubato* written in the score (Exx. 289, 290). Because of the written appoggiatura G-sharp on the first beat

Ex. 289. Op. 22, II, 18-20

Ex. 290. Op. 31/1, II, 5-6, 9

of measure 6 of Op. 31/1, II (Ex. 290), the three appoggiaturas in measure 5 could logically be played on the beat. The low C-natural in measure 9 could be played on the beat as part of the ascending trill. In Op. 49/2, II, the appoggiatura in measure 28 forms a broken chord which enters *forte* and, therefore, seems to belong on the beat (Ex. 291).

Ex. 291. Op. 49/2, II, 27-28

Certain single appoggiaturas seem to belong on the beat and to be accented because of the dissonance which they introduce (Exx. 292, 293).

Ex. 292. Op. 31/3, I, 18-21

Ex. 293. Op. 53, I, 4

*Appoggiaturas which stand alone, without any accompanying voices against which they may be placed.* When a long main note follows, it is difficult to hear the appoggiatura as accented and "on the beat" (Ex. 294). The upbeat effect of the D-natural appoggiatura is balanced by the stress of a heavy beat on the G-natural in the following measure. The accent placed over the main note makes the

Ex. 294. Op. 2/1, I, 41-43

appoggiatura sound as though it were ahead of the beat, no matter how much the appoggiatura may be delayed by the performer (Ex. 295).

Ex. 295. Op. 7, III, 35-38

The examples which Clementi gives in his *Introduction* consistently show the appoggiatura played on the beat. Czerny, in the *Piano School,* seems less sure of himself. As noted earlier, he directs that an appoggiatura standing before a chord or before double notes must be played with the remainder of the chord or with the lower note, as the case may be, while the note to which the appoggiatura belongs follows immediately afterward. He continues:

> From all these Examples the Pupil will perceive, that the small notes do not in the least disturb the measure; since the *Accent,* which each full sized note must receive according to its value, always remains with the large note, just as though the preceding note was not there at all.[22]

According to Czerny's description, the appoggiatura becomes a real "crushed note," or *acciaccatura.*

In summary, if there is a choice with respect to the exact position of the appoggiatura in relation to the beat, it might be preferable to reserve the appoggiatura on the beat for slow movements and the one ahead of the beat for moderate or fast movements. Since the time which an appoggiatura played on the beat takes from the main note introduces the effect of *rubato* written in the score, a decision can come only after much playing of the passage in question.

Compound appoggiaturas found in the Beethoven sonatas include inverted turns, slides, broken chords and arpeggiated chords. Beethoven's usage with respect to inverted turns and slides seldom

permits anything but an execution beginning on the beat. There are
exceptions in which a figure resembling a snapped turn would almost
certainly be played ahead of the beat before which it stands (Exx.
296, 297). In the passage from ·Op. 81a (Ex. 296), Beethoven
would probably have indicated a trill, as he did in measure 18, if he
had wanted the ornament in measure 16 to be played on the second
eighth-note beat. After all the activity in measure 17, he may have
wanted the G-natural at the beginning of measure 18 to be a longer
note.

Ex. 296. Op. 81a, II, 15-19

Ex. 297. Op. 109, III, 6

In contrast, the compound appoggiatura in the form of an inverted turn in Exx. 298-302 must be played on the beat. As a result,
the main note is displaced and the beat may even be slightly
lengthened. This rhythmic adjustment supports the opinion that
"free rhythm," to a great extent, is written in the score. In each of
these cases the compound appoggiatura is prevented by a preceding
rhythmic figure from being played ahead of the beat.

Ex. 298. Op. 2/1, I, 7-8

Ex. 299. Op. 7, II, 62-64

Ex. 300. Op. 7, IV, 4-5

Ex. 301. Op. 10/2, I, 9-12

Ex. 302. Op. 13, II, 21-23

In addition to the examples above, the compound appoggiatura in measure 24 of the slow movement of Op. 2/1 should probably be played on the beat with the D-natural (Ex. 303).

Ex. 303. Op. 2/1, II, 23-24

Certain rhythmic figures preceding compound appoggiaturas in the form of slides determine that the appoggiatura must be played on the beat (Exx. 304, 305).

Ex. 304. Op. 49/1, II, 2-4

Ex. 305. Op. 110, I, 4

In Op. 13, III, and Op. 31/1, II, the slide should probably be played on the beat (Exx. 306, 307).

Ex. 306. Op. 13, III, 4-8

Ex. 307. Op. 31/1, II, 33-34

Because of the two distinct articulation slurs, a realization before the beat for the slide in Op. 13, III (Ex. 306), seems incorrect (Ex. 308). In this instance and that from the slow movement of Op. 31/1 (Ex. 307), the slide may be heard as having the effect of being one note.

Ex. 308.

In Op. 7, II, an instance occurs of a slide written as a compound appoggiatura and, in the same measure, others written in large notation. Standing as it does in an uncrowded situation (in contrast to the examples of the slide given above) and leading to a main note marked with a *sforzando,* the compound appoggiatura in measure 64 should no doubt be played unaccented and ahead of the beat (Ex. 309).

Ex. 309. Op. 7, II, 63-65

For the purpose of this paper, a broken chord is defined as one that is not notated to be held down (Ex. 310a), while an arpeggiated chord is defined as one which is held from the bottom note to the top as a rolled chord (Ex. 310b).

Ex. 310a.     Ex. 310b.

Both Czerny and Clementi give directions for the playing of compound appoggiaturas in the form of broken chords, although they do not agree. According to Czerny, all

> ... Appoggiaturas consisting of several small notes, must always be played so quick, as not to take away from the following large notes, any position either of their accent or their duration; nor must they in any respect disturb the measure, nor the distribution of the notes.[23]

The examples which Czerny provides include both slides and broken chords (Ex. 311). Clementi's examples illustrating the execution

Ex. 311.

etc.

of compound appoggiaturas of this type show the small notes receiving a reasonable portion of the beat (Ex. 312).[24]

Ex. 312.

As usual, Beethoven's usage of the device varies. In Op. 10/3, II, a clear-cut illustration occurs of such a figure beginning on the beat. It may be more accurate to say that the ear hears a delayed first beat with the Bb-D third in the right hand, marked *forte,* coinciding with the *fp* G in the left hand (Ex. 313).

Ex. 313. Op. 10/3, II, 35-36

In Op. 10/1, III, both the arpeggiated chord in the left hand and the broken chord in the right hand would probably be played together, the *ffp* defining the beginning of the beat (Ex. 314).

Ex. 314. 10/1, III, 20-23

By placing the *Tempo I* and the *fortissimo* at the beginning of the broken chord later in the same movement, Beethoven insists that the figure give the effect of beginning on the beat (Ex. 315).

Ex. 315. Op. 10/1, III, 113-115

In each of the three preceding examples (although to a lesser degree in the second), the measure in which the broken chord appears is lengthened. Therefore the broken chord, like other compound appoggiaturas, may be considered a written "free tempo" device. It follows that in any movement marked *espressivo* broken chords should be begun where the beat would ordinarily fall, resulting in a displacement of the beat or a readjustment of the rhythmic pulse of the passage. The theme of the last movement of Op. 109 bears such a marking; in measure 14 the broken chord in the right hand is notated to be begun after the arpeggiated chord (according to our definition) in the left hand. One could assume that the broken chords in measures 5 and 13 would be begun with the note or notes

in the left hand on the first beat, creating the effect of expanding
the beat (Ex. 316). At the last statement of the theme at the end

Ex. 316. Op. 109, III, 4-5, 13-14

of the movement, the *crescendo-decrescendo* in measures 4 and 5 is
missing, and the E-major chord in measure 5 is no longer broken.
In the manuscript, the F-sharp minor broken chord in measure 13
is also a solid chord in the last statement of the theme, although in
the original edition it appears as in Ex. 316. These modifications
suggest that the character of the theme has changed, so that the
movement does not end exactly as it began but rather has become
simpler, less *espressivo*.

Even when convinced of the association of broken chords with
free tempo or *rubato,* the fact remains that such a conclusion is
in the nature of intelligent speculation. One cannot be certain
exactly how Beethoven conceived such passages. If, in Op. 10/1,
I, each broken chord is played on the beat, a slight break is introduced which separates the two-measure phrases from each other
and from the four-measure phrase which begins in measure 13.
The holding back in tempo increases until measure 13, after which
a more fluent pace is again found (Ex. 317). In Op. 27/2, III, it

Ex. 317. Op. 10/1, I, 9-16

would seem preferable to begin the broken chord on the beat simultaneously with the beginning of the same harmony in the Alberti
bass figure in the left hand (Ex. 318).

Ex. 318. Op. 27/2, III, 60-62

Czerny was disturbed by an excessive use of arpeggiated chords. In his discussion of situations most suitable for this treatment, he begins by saying,

> Many players accustom themselves so much to Arpeggio chords, that they at last become quite unable to strike full chords or even double notes firmly and at once; this latter way is the general rule, while the former constitutes the exception.[25]

He continues by recommending that chords made up of very short notes, chords which are supposed to be played with a great deal of power, and chords which are formed by contrapuntal writing should not be arpeggiated. Beethoven's performance practice of rolled chords which are to be played very powerfully is just the opposite (Exx. 319-323).

Ex. 319. Op. 2/1, I, 7-8

Ex. 320. Op. 7, II, 64

Ex. 321. Op. 10/1, II, 44-47

Ex. 322. Op. 10/3, II, 7-8

Ex. 323. Op. 57, II, 96-97

In Op. 57, II, the arpeggio signs in measures 96-97 in the manuscript differ from those in the *Gesamtausgabe* (Ex. 323). According to the manuscript, in measure 96 the sign should continue unbroken from the lowest note in the left hand to the highest in the right, while in the next measure Beethoven wrote *arpeggio* under the left-hand chord, with the appropriate sign, and *secco* under the chord in the right-hand, without the arpeggio sign.

Arpeggiated chords are treated according to the requirements of the passage in which they are found.

> In arpeggioing, the single notes may not only be played so extremely fast, that the arpeggoied chord shall almost resemble a chord struck plain; but they may also be played slower and slower, in every possible gradation, down to that degree in which each single note will be equal in duration to a crotchet in a slow time; we must measure and apply these different degrees, exactly according as the chord is to be held down long or quickly detached, and struck either piano and smorzando, or forte and hard[26]

The example which Czerny then introduces shows that he was thinking of the D-minor Sonata, Op. 31/2, which he studied with Beethoven (Ex. 324).

Ex. 324.

Of this example Czerny writes:

> Here the single notes of the arpeggioed chords must fol-
> low one another extremely slow, *and we only begin to count
> the time prescribed from the last and highest note.*[27]

Czerny adds that we are entitled to this extension of the time,
"as the passage forms a sort of pause."[28]

It is interesting that Czerny speaks of measuring the value of
the single notes of arpeggiated chords. In some instances Beethoven
wrote a measured arpeggiated chord (Exx. 325-327). In Op. 22,
IV, and in Op. 57, I, the *arpeggio* is notated to begin on the beat
(Exx. 325, 327), while in Op. 27/2, III, the effect seems to be that
of preceding the beat (Ex. 326).

Ex. 325. Op. 22, IV, 22-24

Ex. 326. Op. 27/2, III, 163-164

Ex. 327. Op. 57, I, 123-126

# Notes and Sources

## Chapter VI

[1]From the facsimile of the autograph, published by the Beethoven House in Bonn.

[2]Carl Czerny, *Complete Theoretical and Practical Piano Forte School* (London, 1839), Vol. I, p. 172.

[3]Carl Philipp Emanuel Bach, *Essay on the True Art of Playing Keyboard Instruments,* translated and edited by William J. Mitchell (New York: W. W. Norton & Company, 1949), p. 118.

[4]*Ibid.,* pp. 110-112.

[5]Friedrich Wilhelm Marpurg, *Anleitung zum Clavierspielen* (Berlin, 1765), p. 56.

[6]Daniel Gottlob Türk, *Klavierschule* (Leipzig und Halle, 1789), p. 274.

[7]Muzio Clementi, *Introduction to the Art of Playing the Pianoforte* (London, 180?), p. 11.

[8]Carl Czerny, *Vollständige theoretisch-practische Pianoforte-Schule, Op. 500* (Vienna: Diabelli u. Comp., 1942), Vol. IV, p. 56.

[9]Bach, p. 105.

[10]Czerny, *Piano Forte School,* Vol. I, p. 171.

[11]Bach, p. 114.

[12]*Ibid.,* p. 118.

[13]Czerny, *Piano Forte School,* Vol. I, p. 165.

[14]*Ibid.,* Vol. IV, p. 55.

[15]Bach, pp. 121, 126.

[16]Türk, pp. 220-222.

[17]Bach, p. 92.

[18]Czerny, *Pianoforte-Schule,* Vol. IV, p. 94.
[19]Czerny, *Piano Forte School,* Vol. I, p. 160.
[20]Czerny, *Pianoforte-Schule,* Vol. IV, p. 44.
[21]Bach, p. 123.
[22]Czerny, *Piano Forte School,* Vol. I, p. 161.
[23]*Ibid.,* p. 162.
[24]Clementi, *Introduction.*
[25]Czerny, *Piano Forte School,* Vol. III, p. 55.
[26]*Ibid.,* p. 56.
[27]*Ibid.*
[28]*Ibid.*

# VII

## *A Point of Reference*

IN AN ESSAY entitled "The Creative Process," James Baldwin describes the quality of "aloneness" in the artist — not in the sense of solitude found in some remote place in the wild, but the aloneness of particular events in human life, such as birth, suffering and death. The business of the artist, Mr. Baldwin writes, is to lay bare the questions which have been hidden by answers.[1]

Unlike the artist of James Baldwin's essay, the musician of the present day tends to believe in the finality of answers. The use of Urtext editions, research into performance practices of the past, the right piano sound, the correct interpretation learned from an accepted authority, the recognition gained by winning a competition, the surface perfection possible with modern mechanics of recording — all provide varying degrees of validity which may be used to conquer insecurity and offer protection from criticism. To be sure, there is nothing wrong with using an Urtext edition, or researching ornamentation, or practicing to play as cleanly as possible. Quite to the contrary, such answers are absolutely essential. The danger lies in forgetting the original question which aroused the uncertainty.

It is easily forgotten that the score is already an answer to a problem in the composer's mind, namely, how to commit to musical notation the expressive possibilities of his material, whether this material is a particular sound, a melodic or rhythmic pattern, a technical figure, or a combination of all three. Of course, no notation

196

can definitively express a subjective experience, nor can any set of rules regulate completely the playing of the notation which the composer finally chose. However vital it may be to reproduce the written page as accurately as possible, the quality of subjective meaning which the patterns in the score had for the composer's imagination, or has for the performer's imagination, determines the difference between art and empty display.

Familiarity with the external side of the music may contribute to a false sense of comprehension. When one prepares a recital premiering works of contemporary composers, formal landmarks are not immediately evident, tonal lyricism is often missing, and technical patterns may be unlike anything encountered before. In such a situation there is no choice but to find the point of reference within one's experience, basing judgments upon intuition alone. Is it a good work? If so, why? In seeking to make the music intelligible, the performer is forced to understand problems of composition, such as the role of form as a logical means of continuity in music (rather than a system of labels for identifying sections of the work), or the structural implication of every sort of contrast — not just the contrast of soft and loud or major and minor, but contrasts in the exploitation of technical patterns, the registers of the instrument, or the speed at which new ideas appear. For example, the pendulum motion of the first measures of Webern's *Variations,* which results from the use of the tone row in retrograde, becomes the means of continuity throughout the movement, extending also to the serializing of dynamics and note values. The ABA form of the movement is delineated by the quicker rhythmic activity of the middle section, crowding the forward-backward statements into smaller segments of time.

Beethoven was once a contemporary composer also. It is difficult to imagine a time when the point of reference for studying a new work by Beethoven was not to be found in a comparison of all the available recordings but rather in personal judgments unaided by accepted guidelines. If there were nothing in one's previous listening experience with which to compare the music, understanding and judging such a work would be a far more personal matter. Most considered his music original, but many also thought it too difficult, unnatural, labored and artificial. Moscheles' teacher, for example, warned his ten-year-old student that if he were ever caught learning a work of Beethoven, he could find another teacher, because Beethoven "writes lots of crazy stuff, — leads the student astray."[2] It seemed to be music calculated to produce effects which would stimulate psychological states rather than to fulfil the conditioned expectations of the contemporary mind. To many the ordering of ideas seemed too disjointed and the changes of direction too violent. Others, who were unprepared to accept the subjective experience of tempo and the primitive quality of dynamic contrast as legitimate interest sustaining elements, found the demands which length and content placed upon the listener's concentration excessive. For the present-day musician the subjective treatment of tempo is probably most baffling. Neither the choice of tempo, nor modifications of the chosen tempo, would have been considered an arbitrary matter by Beethoven, whose performance remained consistent with the inner force of his subjective impulses. Because this need to be consistent with a subjective sense of musical rightness was part of Beethoven's original creative act, the performer cannot evade the same involvement when recreating the score. To the extent that the impact of the music depends upon tempo — or dynamics — the performer becomes the work. Whether the music succeeds or fails rests in the final moment within him, alone.

This is not to suggest that unbridled individualism is the answer to the interpretation of Beethoven. In the *Death in Venice,* Thomas Mann writes that the path to truth for the artist is over the sensuous and that the sensuous is an abyss which impels the artist to develop ever greater discipline. Every modification of the tempo, whether it is a *meno mosso,* a *ritenuto,* an *accelerando,* or a dramatic pause, must be based on an intelligent, thorough understanding of formal aspects of the piece. The first movement of Op. 110 may be used as an example. Following the quasi-introductory opening, the exposition of the movement proceeds by means of continuous variation. The *crescendo* to a sudden *piano* draws attention to the thinness of the two-voice writing in measure 20, at which point the piece begins to move from a structural pitch C-natural to B-flat. Since the recapitulation, rather than being a literal repeat of the exposition, is expanded by further development in the form of a digression to E-major, Beethoven evidently decided to use the traditional development section as a sequential transition between two untraditional development sections, the exposition and recapitulation. If this explanation is accepted, the repetitive directness of the middle section should be played straightforwardly, without any fussiness calculated to make it more "interesting," while the expansive nature of the outer sections seems to require "free performance" — holding back the tempo at the entrance of the thirty-seconds in measure 12 (Czerny's "transition into another species of time"), a pause to accommodate the *subito piano* in measure 20, and a *ritenuto* to avoid hurrying the thirty-seconds in measure 69 — not to mention Beethoven's own *ritenente* in measure 78. Free performance is not really "free." It is an interpretive responsibility to making musical sense.

Besides submitting mentally to the musical sense of the piece, the pianist submits to the physical discipline of playing the notes and of observing phrasing and indications of touch and dynamics. Because thought is carried out in terms of physical movement, either real or imagined, the act of performance, by translating the patterns and directions of the printed page into hand positions, phrasing and touches, recreates the composer's own physical movements to produce the sounds he heard in his imagination. Thus the physical experience of playing Beethoven brings the performer into Beethoven's mind as realistically as his intellectual involvement of following the progress of the composer's thought through analytical study. Schindler singles out as the cause for the neglect of Beethoven's works the general preference for elegance and virtuoso display in the music of Hummel and others of his type,[3] and Czerny remarks that Beethoven, especially in his later years, "paid little attention to a comfortable manner of playing, normal fingering and the like." Czerny continues:

As a rule, his works are just as little suited for the earlier youth, since they make demands not only upon mental but also physical power and since in actuality very little is beneficial or useful if one sees little children (even so-called prodigies) torment themselves with these works.[4]

Of the first movement of Op. 111 in particular, Czerny wrote:

This first movement of the last sonata by Beethoven belongs to the most magnificent and must be played with all power, bravura, and passionate excitement, which the tragic character — as well as the difficulty of the passages — demands.[5]

The technical difficulty is therefore part of the expressiveness of the piece. This does not imply that the pianist with less technical ability will be a better Beethoven interpreter because his "struggle

level" is lower. On the contrary, the uncomfortable writing in Beethoven demands the finest technical effort of which a pianist is
capable. The implication would seem to be that facilitations (Exx.
328-331) should be avoided, since the struggle involved in wrestling
with the physical difficulty is audible evidence of inner effort to
achieve some desired goal.

Ex. 328. Op. 57, I, 13-14

Ex. 329. Op. 106, I, 1

Ex. 330. Op. 109, I, 9

Ex. 331. Op. 111, I, 1

Neither should a *crescendo-subito piano* be weakened by a
*diminuendo,* as Moscheles so frequently indicated in his edition of
the Sonatas. Likewise, phrasing which impedes the even flow or
the sweep of the rhythm should not be altered for convenience in
performance. If articulation slurs are played as drop-lift figures,
the forward thrust of the rhythm and consequently the tempo is held
back (Exx. 332-338). The dotted figure in the opening measure

Ex. 332. Op. 10/1, III, 1-2

Ex. 333. Op. 26, II, 1-4

Ex. 334. Op. 31/3, I, 1

of Op. 31/3 loses its *portamento* quality if the sixteenth is treated as an anticipation of the note it precedes (Ex. 334a), rather than

Ex. 334a.

as a note which is lifted out of the dotted eighth (Ex. 334b). True

Ex. 334b.

to the character of *Das Lebewohl,* the opening statement of the *Allegro* of Op. 81a is held back in tempo by complex phrasing movements (Ex. 335). At a point later in the movement Beethoven ex-

Ex. 335. Op. 81a, I, 17-19

plicitly directs a phrasing lift before the *sforzando* G-flat and then the G-natural, producing the expressive effect of an outward reaching gesture done with great effort and energy (Ex. 336). Similarly,

Ex. 336. Op. 81a, I, 35-38

the opening of the first movement of **Op.** 90 loses much of its impact if the two-note slur is extended into the eighth-note E. Beethoven's slurring requires that the F-sharp be played as though it were pulled away from the dotted-quarter G (Ex. 337). Beethoven must have

Ex. 337. Op. 90, I, 1-4

heard it thus, considering his development of fragmentary motives throughout the exposition (Exx. 338a, 338b). Finally, the theme

Ex. 338a. Op. 90, I, 47-50

Ex. 338b. Op. 90, I, 61-64

of the Rondo of the E-flat Concerto (Ex. 339) is often played

Ex. 339. Op. 73, III, 1-2

without any regard for the two-note slurs and the intense cross-rhythm these produce (Ex. 339a).

Ex. 339a.

The intellectual discipline of understanding the composer's options and choices and the physical discipline of complying with the execution indicated by his directions require a lengthy period of study. Beyond these is a philosophical discipline, less easily perceived and often ignored, which demands continuing personal growth and a capacity for reflection. To resolve that no Beethoven sonata, not even the most brilliant outwardly, will be misused as a display piece is laudable, although the thoughtful interpreter, the one who possibly comes nearest the spirit of Beethoven, will go further, eventually finding the same resigned state of mind which no longer needs approbation or even an audience. The basically introspective, yet self-forgetting, quality apparent in a movement such as the Variations of Op. 109 or the Arietta of Op. 111 cannot be taught. It is perhaps only to be learned outside the studio, through involvement in whatever capacity in the needs of human beings.

To the degree that he senses the composer's presence in the music — whether it is as the formal tactician, the indomitable combatant, or the solitary contemplating the ultimate aloneness — the artist recognizes within himself an objective judge to whom technical and interpretive questions may be referred. This involvement with questions is a lifelong process of study, practice, performing, relearning and finding new meaning, to which the usual answers of the professional world in which one searches for success are by comparison only of incidental importance.

# Notes and Sources

## Chapter VII

[1]James Baldwin, *The Creative Process* (in *Creative America,* published for The National Cultural Center. New York: The Ridge Press, 1962), pp. 17-21.

[2]Alfred Christian Kalischer, *Beethoven und seine Zeitgenossen* (Berlin and Leipzig, 1909-1910), Vol. IV (*Ignaz Moscheles' Verkehr mit Beethoven*), p. 44.

[3]Anton Schindler, *Beethoven as I Knew Him,* edited by Donald W. MacArdle (Chapel Hill: The University of North Carolina Press, 1966), pp. 161-162.

[4]Carl Czerny, *Vollständige theoretisch-practische Pianoforte-Schule, Op. 500* (Vienna, 1842), Vol. IV, p. 33.

[5]Czerny, *Pianoforte-Schule,* Vol. IV, p. 69.

# *Bibliography*

Emily Anderson, *The Letters of Beethoven*. New York: St. Martin's Press, 1961. London: Macmillan & Co.

Carl Philipp Emanuel Bach, *Essay on the True Art of Playing Keyboard Instruments,* translated and edited by William J. Mitchell. New York: W. W. Norton & Company, 1949.

Paul and Eva Badura-Skoda, *Interpreting Mozart on the Keyboard*. London: Barrie and Rockliff, 1962.

Edward Bellasis, *Cherubini: Memorials Illustrative of His Life*. London, 1874.

Gerhard von Breuning, *Aus dem Schwarzspanierhause*. Vienna, 1874.

Hans von Bülow (ed.), *Beethoven Sonatas*. New York: G. Schirmer, 1894.

Hans von Bülow (ed.), *Cramer: Fifty Studies*. New York: G. Schirmer, 1899.

Ernst Cassirer, *The Question of Jean-Jacques Rousseau*. Bloomington: Indiana University Press, 1963.

Muzio Clementi, *Introduction to the Art of Playing the Piano Forte*. London, 180?.

Ernest Closson, *History of the Piano*. London: Paul Elek, 1947.

*Creative America*. New York: The Ridge Press, Inc., 1962.

Carl Czerny, *Complete Theoretical and Practical Piano Forte School*. London, 1839.

Carl Czerny, *Ueber den richtigen Vortrag der Sämtlichen Beethoven'schen Klavierwerke*. Vienna: Universal Edition, 1963.

Carl Czerny, *Vollständige theoretisch-practische Pianoforte-Schule, Op. 500*. Vienna, 1842.

Albert Dreetz, *Czerny und Beethoven.* Leipzig: Kistner & Siegel, 1932.

*Encyclopaedia Britannica.* New York, 1911. Chicago, 1958.

Theodor von Frimmel, *Beethoven Studien.* Munich and Leipzig, 1904-1906.

Ronald Gray (ed.), *Poems of Goethe.* Cambridge: University Press, 1966.

Anna Gertrud Huber, *Beethovens Ammerkungen zu einer Auswahl von Cramer-Etuden.* Zurich: Hug & Company, 1961.

Anna Gertrud Huber, *Ludwig van Beethoven, Seine Schüler und Interpreten.* Vienna: Walter Krieg, 1953.

Johann Nepomuk Hummel, *A Complete Theoretical and Practical Course of Instruction in the Art of Playing the Piano Forte.* London, 1827.

Alfred Christian Kalischer, *Beethoven und seine Zeitgenossen.* Berlin and Leipzig, 1909-1910.

Friedrich Kerst, *Beethoven: The Man and the Artist, as Revealed in his own Words,* translated and edited by Henry Edward Krehbiel. New York: Dover Publications, 1964.

Arthur Loesser, *Men, Women and Pianos.* New York: Simon and Schuster, 1954.

Donald MacArdle, *Anton Felix Schindler, Friend of Beethoven. Music Review,* Vol. 24, No. 1. February, 1963.

Adolf Bernhard Marx, *Anleitung zum Vortrag Beethovenscher Klavierwerke.* Berlin, 1875.

Paul Mies, *Textkritische Untersuchungen bei Beethoven.* Bonn: Beethoven House, 1957.

Charlotte Moscheles, *Life of Moscheles.* London, 1873.

Ignaz Moscheles (ed.), *Beethoven Sonatas.* Leipzig: Hallberger, 1858.

Paul Nettl, *Beethoven Encyclopedia.* New York: Philosophical Library, 1956.

Gustav Nottebohm, *Beethoveniana.* Leipzig and Winterthur, 1872.

Gustav Nottebohm, *Zweite Beethoveniana.* Leipzig, 1887.

Roy Pascal, *The German Sturm und Drang.* New York: Philosophical Library, 1953.

Heinrich Schenker and Erwin Ratz (ed.), *Beethoven Klaviersonaten.* Vienna: Universal Edition, 1947.

Ludwig Schiedermair, *Der Junge Beethoven.* Leipzig: Quelle & Meyer, 1925.

Anton Schindler, *Beethoven as I Knew Him,* edited by Donald W. MacArdle and translated by Constance S. Jolly. Chapel Hill: The University of North Carolina Press, 1966. London: Faber and Faber, Ltd.

Artur Schnabel (ed.), *Beethoven Sonatas.* New York: Simon and Schuster, 1935.

Harold Schonberg, *The Great Pianists.* New York: Simon and Schuster, 1963.

O. G. Sonneck, *Beethoven: Impressions by his Contemporaries.* New York: Dover Publications, 1967.

Friedrich Starke, *Wiener Piano-Forte Schule.* Vienna, 1820.

Nicholas Temperly, *Tempo and Repeats in the Early Nineteenth Century. Music and Letters,* Vol. 47, No. 4. October, 1966.

*Thayer's Life of Beethoven,* revised and edited by Elliot Forbes. Princeton: Princeton University Press, 1967; Princeton Paperback, 1970.

Donald Francis Tovey and Harold Craxton (ed.), *Beethoven Sonatas.* London: Associated Board of the Royal Schools of Music, 1931.

Daniel Gottlob Türk, *Klavierschule.* Leipzig and Halle, 1789.

Alan Tyson, *Moscheles and his 'Complete Edition' of Beethoven. Music Review,* Vol. 25, No. 2. May, 1964.

B. A. Wallner and Conrad Hansen (ed.), *Beethoven Klavier-Sonaten.* München-Duisburg: G. Henle Verlag, 1952.

Franz Gerhard Wegler and Ferdinand Ries, *Biographische Notizen über Ludwig van Beethoven.* Coblenz, 1838.

# The Sonatas of Beethoven

Bonn Sonata in E♭, WoO 47: I-9.

Trio, Op. 1/2: II—178.

Sonata, Op. 2/1: 36; I—45, 68, 108, 120, 183-184, 191; II—95, 173-174, 181, 186; III—168, 177; IV—54, 86, 128, 169, 172

Sonata, Op. 2/2: 36; I—18, 56, 59-60, 62, 119, 155-156, 179; II—128; IV—8-9, 128, 135, 180.

Sonata, Op. 2/3: 36; I—17, 47, 56, 116, 153, 168-169, 171; II— 55, 71-72, 117, 156; III—96-97; IV—17, 45-46, 61-62, 118, 169.

Sonata, Op. 7: 36; I—108, 171; II—55-57, 99, 186-188, 191; III—108-109, 153-154, 183-184; IV—46, 60, 99, 109, 158-160, 186.

Sonata, Op. 10/1: 36; I—107-108, 190; II—64, 109-110, 115, 158, 160, 172-173, 191; III—52, 68, 102, 110, 189, 200.

Sonata, Op. 10/2: 37; I—62, 181, 186; II—177; III—95.

Sonata, Op. 10/3: 37; I—12, 66, 96, 110-111, 178; II—6, 42, 53, 66-67, 119-120, 173, 188-189, 192; IV—45-46, 62-63, 173, 177.

Sonata, Op. 13: 10-11, 21, 37, 106; I—43, 51, 64, 95-97, 107-108, 112, 120-121, 132, 157, 180; II—48, 51-52, 186; III—127, 181, 187.

Sonata, Op. 14/1: 21, 37; I—86, 129; III—85, 97.

Sonata, Op. 14/2: 21, 37; I—92-93, 129; II—42; III—180.

Concerto, Op. 15: 21; III—124.

Sonata, Op. 22; 37; I—30, 62-63, 171-172; II—55, 114, 132, 182; IV—193.

Sonata, Op. 26: 38, 159; I—54, 87-88, 115, 128, 137, 144; II—83, 201; III—42, 132, 144; IV—43, 88-89, 118.

Sonata, Op. 27/1: 38, 159; I—98, 152; II—42, 126; III—48, IV—70, 83.

Sonata, Op. 27/2: 24, 38, 159; I—6, 48-49, 66, 79-80, 89, 117, 142, 160; III—57, 66, 79-80, 96, 126-127, 190-191, 193.

Sonata, Op. 28: 38; I—47, 49, 58, 98, 120, 144; II—21, 43, 54, 98, 179; III—123; IV—49, 131.

Sonata, Op. 31/1: 38-39; I—98, 100-102, 127, 156; II—54, 134, 176, 183, 187.